BETTER BUSINESS ON PURPOSE

MAKE MONEY. CREATE IMPACT.
BE A FORCE FOR GOOD.

Nikki Gatenby, Tim Healey
and Neil Witten

"We've spent trillions fucking up the future, why can't we spend billions on sorting it out?"

Cameron Herold

Welcome, brave visionary

Better Business On Purpose is an inspirational, practical guide for those of us that want to make money and create an impact, so you and your business are a force for good.

→ Are you a founder with soul, who wants to create a legacy for future generations?

→ You may be a business owner with many years trading, or perhaps a new company in start-up mode.

→ You could be an ethical business junkie who wants to absorb best practice so you can feed it into the mix where you work.

→ Perhaps you find yourself within a corporate machine, and your sole purpose is to rebel to create positive lasting change?

As we see it, whoever you are, buying this book is a huge step in the right direction.

It shows you care. It shows you believe that you and your business can do 'more', can 'give back', and leave a legacy.

In this book we will guide you through the thinking behind being a Better Business On Purpose (a BBOP), and the process of how to become one.

We recognise that it can be really tough finding the time and resource to be a BBOP. Many of us find that just the day-to-day running of our own businesses can be all consuming.

If you're in any way unsure as to whether you should embark on this journey of discovery, ask yourself these questions:

→ Are you running your business or is it running you?

→ Do you talk about your company and its legacy with pride?

→ Do you wish that you could get off the eternal treadmill of the everyday and be more of a Better Business On Purpose?

→ Do you want to balance making money with creating impact and being a force for good in the world?

We believe that business without purpose is just admin. Your business has the potential to be so much more than that.

If you are ready to make yours a Better Business On Purpose, and want to learn how, then this is most definitely the book for you.

Big profits, bigger impact

There are plenty of business books out there and only so many hours in the day. So why should you read ours? We're biased, of course, but we think this book has the potential to radically change the way you lead, for the better.

The thing is, most business books ask you to pick a lane. There are shelves full of books which will teach you how to develop a business that will make lots of money. And there are others (fewer, but still loads) which explain how to build an ethical business that will create meaningful impact.

Why should you have to choose?

Businesses need to make money in a consistent and sustainable way in order to survive and thrive. Let's not be shy about that. But businesses also have the potential to be a force for good in the world, to benefit people, communities and the planet.

There aren't many books that balance the two, that don't prioritise either profit or purpose at the expense of the other. That's why we've written Better Business On Purpose. To help you do both. On purpose.

After reading this book, we believe that your approach to your company will evolve beyond the day-to-day trouble-shooting and management of running a great business.

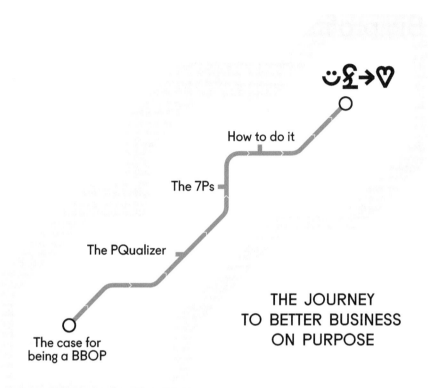

THE JOURNEY
TO BETTER BUSINESS
ON PURPOSE

Using our provided framework, you'll be able to implement positive change and you'll feel more confident having those conversations that challenge the status quo.

1. Inspired by our case studies and guided by 'how to guides', you will launch new initiatives that drive impact, becoming a force for good both internally (within your business) and externally (outside your business), while also making money.

2. For board meetings and a more 'helicopter view', we will introduce you to the PQualizer – our own visual representation of company performance viewed through a BBOP lens. This simple system will help

you to assess where your business is – on its journey to become a BBOP – and how to track your progress.

3. We'll introduce you to the 7 levers at any company's disposal to optimise your business as a BBOP (known as the 7Ps). These 7Ps underpin purpose-led businesses. We will explain why each P matters and see examples of businesses that have got the balance right among all 7Ps (as well as a few that really haven't).

4. We will also unpack the step-by-step process of implementation: becoming a BBOP. We will break it down into bite-size chunks, so that your business can address each P individually and never feel over-loaded. There will be practical advice and direction, as well as inspirational jump-off points, which you can put into action with immediate effect.

This is not a book

OK, technically it is a book, but it's not JUST a book.

It's a mindset for leaders and a movement for businesses. Being a BBOP is all about embracing the agenda for positive change, for all, within a liberal capitalist system.

However, we understand that change doesn't happen by reading a book alone.

To help and support you along your journey, we have made a number of downloadable tools to accompany your journey.

Just grab your phone and use the camera to scan the QR code below, and you'll be able to access our online BBOP Library containing a number of resources:

The PQualizer

To help assess your business and track its progress towards becoming – and then sustaining as – a BBOP, please grab yourself a copy of our PQualizer tool.

Supporting video series

We have created a series of short videos that explore the 7Ps and how to go about implementing change, so you can share the content of this book with colleagues.

Supporting tools

A library of supporting checklists & workbooks for each of the 7Ps can be also be downloaded from the library.

Events

From time to time, we run BBOP gatherings and events, both physical and online, to bring together like-minded businesses and share information. Register your interest to be invited to our next event.

"We need to look at success differently. We need to see the bigger picture; to get to a place where social values are not simply seen as charitable, but as profitable investments, without direct financial outcomes."

ICAS (The Institute of Chartered Accountants of Scotland)

CONTENTS

Meet the authors

NIKKI GATENBY, NEIL WITTEN, TIM HEALEY

Photo credit James Hole

Nikki Gatenby

As author of Amazon Best Seller, *Superengaged: How to transform business performance by putting people and purpose first* , I'm vocal about the need to redress the balance of using people in business in the pursuit of profit. People created business, not the other way around – we do not need to become slaves to the balance sheet. And therein lies the rub, it's all about balance.

I'm an experienced non-exec director and qualified cognitive behavioural coach, having led successful marketing agencies in London, Paris and Brighton, with a track record of taking them global for the past two decades. Having exited my last agency in 2019, I am now an in-demand Agency Specialist Non-Exec Director, working with founders and leaders to make their good agencies great.

I've made a career out of navigating the plate-spinning that comes with leading business and helping others to do the same. It's no longer the time to add more plates but focus on what really matters. Creating better business, on purpose.

Burn out in the agency world is rife. And for such an innovative, creative industry, this is simply wrong. When I took the step to move from London to Brighton, to leave the big smoke and grow an agency based on wellbeing on the south coast of the UK, there were a few raised eyebrows amongst my esteemed big brand colleagues. *'You're doing what?...'*

Roll forward 10 years and we had taken the agency from Brighton to global, from marketing services to developing two successful SaaS technology products that make life better for people in communications (answerthepublic.com and coveragebook.com), hand in hand with the agency being recognised as one of the Best Places to Work in the UK for eight years running. We made plenty of profit to fuel the business, taking no investment on this journey, whilst balancing people and purpose along the way.

Now I'm in a position to help founders and leaders to successfully grow their businesses to fuel their purpose. Bringing a future-facing kind of leadership, courage to assume responsibility for their total world impact – to leave a positive legacy, not a dirty great stain. Profit should not come from creating the world's problems, but by solving them.

I'm not looking for profits with a side of purpose – I'm looking for profits through balancing purpose, positioning, people, product, planet and platforms. More of that throughout the book.

We need to shift our thinking. The human and planetary cost of inertia is significantly higher than the cost of action.

However, change isn't coming from the obvious places, so now it's down to us.

"Embrace the change, or be the dinosaur, shouting at the meteor."

Ian Wright (after the Lionesses
won the Euros in 2022)

Tim Healey

After over 20 years touring the globe as a cutting-edge techno DJ/Music producer and record label owner, I flipped my career and turned my self-taught entrepreneurial skillset to advertising.

Having worked on award-winning projects with Google Creative Labs, YouTube, McCann and a slew of brands from BMW to Disney, I now specialise in strategic marketing as an outsourced Marketing Director. I work directly with CMOs and their teams, from FTSE listed firms to start-ups, to help them get clear on their business vision, purpose, strategy and communications.

I passionately believe that great purpose-led marketing can drive positive behavioural change and contribute to the global movement for greater good. I have seen it happen and been lucky enough to be part of marketing projects that have delivered real social impact.

When I work with businesses, I take a holistic view, one that aims to deliver on a client's business objectives but that also includes the wider positive potential of the business – internally and externally.

I insist that businesses acknowledge the role that they can play in making the world a better place, and then collaborate with them on a marketing strategy that delivers both their desired business results and a lasting legacy.

Many businesses undertake siloed positive activities. Sadly, when these run their course, businesses return to operating as they were, failing to care about their staff or the community sufficiently. I am also acutely aware of a worrying trend: businesses using Corporate Social Responsibility (C.S.R.) as a smoke screen to cover ethically challenging behaviour. Well, no more.

Not on our watch.

For centuries we have taken out more than we put back from our planet – and yet there is another way.

Doing the interviews, the research, and then writing this book with my esteemed colleagues have all helped to crystallise my views on how purpose must be an intrinsic part of every future-facing business.

Embedding purpose as a key pillar within a business, while turning a tidy profit *is* possible. A growing number of businesses all around us are already doing it. Far beyond their economic goals, these companies are attracting the best talent, maximising their operational potential and simultaneously effecting positive societal change.

If this book encourages you to consider how you can run a more ethical, purpose-led company and optimise your business practices, then my co-author colleagues and I will have played our small part in edging the world towards a more positive paradigm. Let's make it happen.

"An adventure is only an inconvenience rightly considered."

G.K. Chesterton

Neil Witten

I started life as a software engineer but realised that I wasn't just into the technology. I was a lot more bothered about the positive impact that technology can have on peoples' lives.

I bootstrapped my first business, Bite Studio, a creative digital agency. It became very profitable. But there were times when it was really tough. Often, we'd worry about making payroll, hiring ahead of the curve, even taking on personal guarantees.

I co-founded my next business, StoryStream, a technology platform for global brands, with investment. We had millions of dollars at our disposal. But it was still really tough. If I learnt just one thing through building those two businesses, it's that however you go about doing it, it's hard. So you need to really care to have the necessary staying power.

We managed to find a way through, and I got to a place where I could 'step back'. I gave myself one year to find whatever felt right.

I stumbled into advising businesses' owners. I realised that by working with one intentional, soulful founder in a short amount of time, we could catalyse meaningful positive change for many (staff, shareholders, partners and customers). That became addictive. So I did more and more of it, but I quickly realised that I couldn't reach everyone on my own. So I started collaborating with people who had previously founded beautiful businesses, and before long, Tim, Nikki and I became three amigos.

One concept really galvanised us: 'beautiful business'.

To understand this, I need to take you right back to when I was 16. I'd landed my first proper job with a software development company, 'Dataline Software', a BBOP through and through.

There were about 20 people, and it was like a family. The two founders were kids of the 60s, hippies at heart, and that manifested deep within the culture. It wasn't about the destination; it was about the journey. Projects were selected based on their meaning and their impact, and not just to the bottom line. People cared.

This was my first proper experience of business, and I loved it. But I also assumed that this was what every business was like. I was wrong.

At the tender age of 29, I had my first 'mid-life crisis' whilst running Bite Studio. I had a great business. My team were fantastic. We were making plenty of money and winning awards. Life was good. But something was wrong. What was the point of all this growth?

I realised that businesses are like art. They can be designed to be beautiful. When they're beautiful, the work they do and the impact they have on peoples' lives is profound.

So after lots of experimentation, I carried on doing what I knew – building technology-based businesses, but with a deliberate edge towards 'beauty'.

As my businesses grew, I saw businesses that were downright ugly. Existing for one reason: to maximise their financial return. Many companies whose products and services I loved, were run by people glued to spreadsheets and emails. Decisions were one dimensional. How does this either make us more money or save us more money?

Deep down I knew what I was being called to do – to help create systemic change. Our world desperately needs it. And that starts with helping soulful founders and business leaders, just like you, who realise that they can build the business they've always dreamed of. One that makes money and creates a positive impact. So the more you do, the better it is for everyone.

Collectively we can create the future that we and future generations so desperately need and deserve.

I love advising founders who are on a journey to create impactful BBOPs. And like most of us I want to create the most positive impact I can. So with Tim and Nikki's help we decided that we should write the book. A book that explains why there's so much potential for positive systemic change coming from soulful founders and business leaders like you. Why the time is now. Why it's actually a safer bet, and a more meaningful one at that.

To be honest, just like me, Better Business On Purpose is probably what you've been searching for. So please see this as an invitation, a licence even. A licence to play by a new rule book.

We hope to reach as many people as possible through this book, and we hope that it's practical and applicable enough that it becomes a catalyst for change in your business and millions of others like yours. So that collectively we can create the future that we and future generations so desperately need and deserve.

"It's not how well you play the game, it's deciding what game you want to play."

Kwame Appiah

"Time is ticking, and we can't wait for the politics to come around and provide the solutions. Businesses can do it today and ought to be leading."

Avi Garbow, Patagonia's Environmental Advocate

You've got soul

The very fact that you have bought this book means you, like us, are also considering the possibilities of a better world, driven by better business.

We know we are not alone. We know there are other business founders, owners and leaders – like you – who 'have soul'. People who care about the trajectory of our modern world, who are shocked by the way mankind has seemingly totalled the planet and disregarded flora, fauna and fellow humans in the search of profit.

Like you, we believe that we all have a duty to play our part in making the world a better place. To put back as much – if not more – than we take out.

There's enough money being made in our world by corporations to address many if not all of the world's major issues. But that isn't happening. Instead, we maximise profit at the expense of all else, ignoring the glaring issues of poverty, lack of sanitation and environmental meltdown.

Well, not all of us. Many are doing great things (you may be one of them yourself) – some of which we'll cover in this book.

We are proposing a radical BBOP approach: one where profit and positive legacy are kept in balance.

From the macro (the global perspective) to the micro (how your business behaves towards your team and suppliers), improvements can be made to your business that will ultimately benefit all; and, crucially, not entirely at the expense of profit, because we recognise that we need profit to operate in our world.

How it began

We came from different backgrounds and with different perspectives: Neil from the technology and entrepreneurial side, Nikki from successful agency leadership with a focus on optimising teams within businesses (having already written a best-seller on this topic), and Tim from a former music producer/DJ turned outsourced marketing director.

As we were based in Brighton, UK, we started by meeting every Wednesday morning for nine months, week in, week out, with an agenda to discuss the possibilities around shaping a world that did 'better business' and quickly established some core principles:

A 'better business' is a business that is optimised on all fronts – operationally and also ethically.

Run correctly, a Better Business On Purpose should make **more** profit, enabling that business to do **more** good.

Furthermore, we could build a network of like-minded business leaders who subscribe to these beliefs.

By sharing their knowledge of successfully run companies, in what we perceive of as a modern, future-facing, planet-conscious way, these leaders and their businesses could play their part in changing the world for the better.

Our often very animated weekly discussions continued as we began to assemble building blocks of what would ultimately be the backbone of our book. We pooled resources, shared our learnings, and avidly read and absorbed research, anecdotes and books by authors also exploring this space. Neil recommended Yancey Strickler's inspirational *This Could Be Our Future: A Manifesto for a More Generous World*, which we all found riveting. Alongside these seemingly alternative business views, we soaked up writing from authors like John Higgs (*The Future Starts Here: An Optimistic Guide to What Comes Next*) and agreed that as a race, as a planet, we have everything to play for, and business can help to set the agenda.

We feel your pain

Early on, we realised that it's not entirely obvious how one might juggle an ethical agenda with a successful business. Even with the best of intentions, it takes all of one's energy just to make sure a business runs well and that your customers are well served.

It happens to the best of us. Indeed, there are times when the survival of your business must be your focus, or your business will fold.

Then there's the deluge of media negativity where one has to dig to find positivity. It is enough to put anyone off embarking on new practices within their company.

We began to assemble case studies of successful examples of positive world events and companies that appeared to be moving towards a BBOP model, in the hope that we could share these stories to support those wanting to make the change.

You wouldn't necessarily know it, but the future's bright

Scroll through your newsfeed, turn on the TV news, or pass any newsagent, and you would be forgiven for feeling a bit queasy.

In their quest to sell papers and keep eyeballs on their apps and rolling news channels, the world's media services are serving up regular portions of brutality, catastrophe and scandal, which add up to a smorgasbord of negativity.

Faced with such a daily diet of doom, it's no surprise that many of us are struggling to look on the bright side. Recent research by the University of Sussex found that consuming negative news exacerbates peoples' own worries, making them unhappier and more anxious. It turns out that bad news is bad for everyone.

But we do have a choice. We can choose to think differently.

We can choose to consume all the bad stuff, or we can seek out positivity, focusing our attention on stories that put heavy-heart events into perspective, and opening our minds to optimistic possibilities. We can make an effort to read and share the good stuff, such as exponential advances in healthcare, education, earnings, technology and quality of life across the globe.

By reacting differently to what we see, we'll train our brains to think differently, shifting from a baseline of *'It's all going to the dogs'* towards one of *'It's all to play for'*. By sharing our perspective, and building businesses that bring this perspective to life, we'll help others do the same, at scale.

A route map to better business

We also quickly established that there is no obvious route map one can follow to optimise a purposeful business. In 2021 we hit upon the idea that one of the most helpful things we could do to contribute to the global movement for greater good was to provide that route map, a 'how to' manual for business leaders who want to do 'more' with their businesses. We also established our passionate belief that, if operated in an ethical and considered way, all businesses would benefit from this approach.

A manual and a movement

Fundamental to our thinking was the creation of movement for change; a deliberate decision taken by business founders and leaders with soul, to base the way they work on meaningful goals, rather than exclusively pursuing financial success. If we could turn more business leaders on to this way of doing business then a growing number of businesses would share this agenda, with the end result being better for the planet.

The 7Ps and the PQualizer

We collectively established the '7Ps'. The concept that a 'Better Business On Purpose' gives equal weight to: purpose; positioning; people; product; profit; planet; platforms (the 7Ps).

It was immediately apparent to all of us, as music lovers, and especially to Tim as a former recording artist and music producer, that a super-simple way to manifest these 7 business levers was for them to be seen as a hi-fi/ stereo separate: a graphic equaliser unit. Remember those? They still exist in studios, and on old home stereo systems, and indeed, if you use iTunes, there is one built in to your app.

For the uninitiated, a stereo graphic equaliser allows you to add or subtract specific audio frequencies from the song that you are listening to. Want more bass or 'low-end sound' on your stereo? No problem; increase the low frequency graphic equaliser above zero. Want less treble? Simply pull the relevant high or treble frequency slider down – into the minus – to taste. Want the middle frequencies to stay as they are? Fine – leave the equaliser on zero.

Just as the graphic equaliser allowed you to adjust your audio, via a number of slider knobs, our 'PQualizer' would be a super-simple way to register how a company was performing. Profit good? Then adjust the profit slider accordingly. If you felt that your company was doing some work on promotion but that its approach to its positioning could improve, maybe that might be on zero. If your business's current attention to the environment and local community was non-existent, then pull the Planet slider below zero.

It was never intended to be scientific – purely a conversational jump-off point for leadership teams to discuss when reviewing company performance. The idea being that this simple graphic representation would promote constructive dialogue within organisations, equipping the user with a schematic tool and reference point for purpose-led conversations.

USE THIS QR CODE TO ACCESS ONLINE VERSIONS OF THE PQUALIZER FOR YOU TO USE.

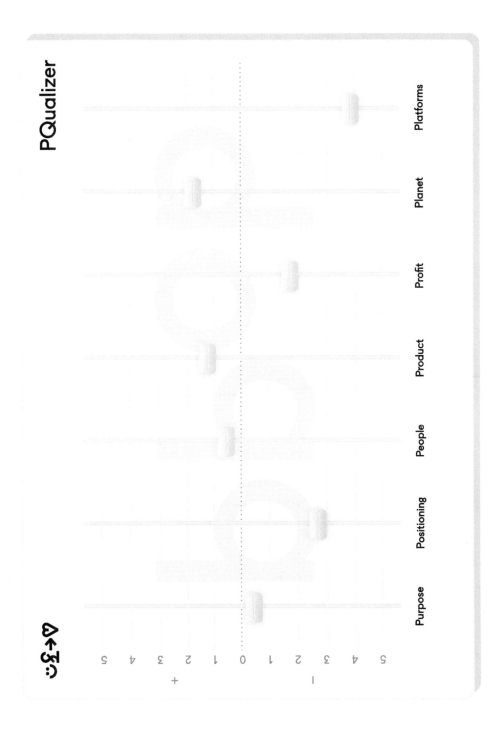

https://seths.blog/

We are not astronomers

Unlike most of the sciences, astronomy is always done at a distance. You can see the stars, but you can't do anything about them.

Sometimes the media would like us to believe that we're all astronomers, simply passive witnesses in a world out of our control.

But the world is never out of our influence.

Remembrance, connection, possibility, invention, empathy, insight, correction, care and justice are all up to us.

We not only observe, but we make changes happen. Our participation (or apathy) leads to a different future.

The ocean is made of drops. And the drops are up to us. Who else is going to care enough to make an impact?

 SETH'S BLOG

How did we get here?

There's a pervading sense out there, not helped by the collective experience of living through a global pandemic, that everything is a bit of a mess. At the time of writing, the Doomsday Clock is set at 100 seconds to midnight. In terms of saving ourselves from destruction, it appears that time is literally running out.

On a specific level, there's also a sense that the business world has gone rogue (it seems that barely a week goes by without a company that was once a 'hero' dropping to 'zero'). That most companies, especially the big ones, are only focused on their bottom line, and that everything, and everyone, that gets in the way is just collateral damage.

Even companies with purpose-led credentials are contributing to this malaise, with all too frequent headlines about the good guys who've gone bad (we won't name names, but we're sure you won't have to think too hard to come up with a few).

Is this really where we are? Do you believe that the pursuit of profit is the only way to run a business? No. Neither do we.

If there is one thing that the pandemic has shown us, it is the importance of taking time to re-evaluate, rethink and reconsider. We are adamant that business leaders who are prepared to shift to different ways of thinking, and doing, have the potential to be a force for good.

This belief was the driving force behind our joint venture; a purpose-focused business consultancy, designed as an antidote to existing models in which spreadsheets and financial maximisation ruled supreme.

No time like the present

Our discussions led us to one conclusion: there is a real possibility that purpose-led businesses could be more agile, innovative and forward thinking than existing governments, and, if aligned, could offer a more positive future for our world.

Around that time, one Sunday morning, we heard historian and journalist Baron Peter Hennessy on Radio 4's *Broadcasting House* programme, talking about how to make the world a better place.

What he said matched our views on the need for purpose-led businesses so closely that we called him up and asked him to tell us more:

> *'We need to look into the depths of possibility that we have amongst ourselves. During the COVID epidemic, we have rediscovered a duty of care for each other, and we have shown immense social solidarity...*
>
> *If we could find a way of concentrating a very considerable part of our best endeavours on five themes, it would ensure two things: that the 2020s are not another wasted decade and secondly that we have a life-long memorial to those that we've lost in this last year. We can turn our dreadful shared experience of COVID into something really good and long-lasting.'*

Peter's five themes were social care, social housing, technical education skills, preparing society and economy for Artificial Intelligence, and mitigating and combating climate change. These are big, important societal issues; how on earth can businesses tackle them?

"Business as usual is not going to be enough. We must act now."

Henrik Poulsen, CEO, Orsted
(under whose watch the company
transformed from fossil fuel to wind power)

Again, Peter has the answer:

> *'We need to fuse liberal capitalism – the best mechanism we have discovered so far for innovation and economic growth – with social democracy – the best way we have discovered for a high level of social justice and redistribution.'*

Indeed, these drivers are shared by our chosen charity, Global Citizen (with which 25% of the profits of our book will be shared).

Join the leaders and founders whose businesses are a force for good

We've written this book, because, like Peter, we believe that by taking the best elements of the business and social spheres, and bringing them together with a clear purpose, founders and leaders can have a sustainable, positive impact on the world, while simultaneously running a successful, profitable enterprise.

We'll explain what Better Business on Purpose is all about and set out the shifts in thinking and doing that will help you be part of the movement. We'll debunk some myths, share some strategies and provide you with some practical tools. And we'll introduce you to the PQualizer, a system we've created to help you get the different aspects of your company in balance and become a force for good.

We'll also provide live examples of organisations who are doing it right. Like Buurtzorg, who challenged the Netherlands' health system's traditional model and radically improved outcomes for patients. Or the challenger banks like Monzo, Revolut, N26 and Starling, who are giving customers ultimate control with a digital bank in their back pockets.

Or Patagonia, who demonstrated their environmental credentials and opposition to disposable high-street fashion by telling customers *'Don't buy this jacket'*.

These organisations, and others who share their values, are thinking differently, acting ethically, and building a Better Business On Purpose. Will you?

BBOP – a definition

So what exactly is a Better Business On Purpose, or a BBOP?

Let's begin by saying what BBOP is *not*.

BBOP is not a certification or badge. There is no examination or strict criteria to adhere to, no award ceremony to pay for, no directory to be listed in.

BBOP is a movement for change, driven by leaders and founders with soul, who have taken a deliberate decision to balance making money with creating impact, and be a force for good.

BBOP is an approach.

BBOP is the belief that business can do better and be better:

- → Better for the planet
- → Better for the local community
- → Better operationally and with technology
- → Better for your partner businesses

→ Better for your team

→ Better for your investors

→ Better for your profit margins

→ And ultimately better for you.

When we say 'a BBOP', we mean a business that is actively attending to the above.

BBOPs come in all shapes and sizes and sit within most sectors.

Every company has the potential to be one, and many are already on the journey to becoming a BBOP, adapting their path as the world around them changes.

Leaders who align with these principles give equal weight to the 7Ps, and can consider their business to be a BBOP:

1. Purpose

2. Positioning

3. People

4. Product

5. Profit

6. Planet

7. Platforms

We'll be digging into these later.

BBOP in action

BBOPs come in all shapes and sizes and sit within most sectors. Every company has the potential to be one, and many are on the journey, adapting their path as the world around them changes.

It's important to remember that being a BBOP doesn't mean getting everything right, or having a perfect score for each of the 7Ps. In fact, it's an occupational hazard of being a purpose-driven founder that it's not always easy to achieve your sky-high standards. And when a BBOP drops a ball, or makes a mistake, the backlash can be fierce – much more so, it could be argued, than when a less purposeful organisation does the same.

So we're not suggesting that the examples we're sharing of BBOP in action are faultless. And they may, at some point in the future, make decisions that actively undermine their BBOP credentials. But they have earned their place in our book because we believe that, on balance, they are acting in a way that makes them a force for good.

Take LEGO, a company that most would agree has an inspirational purpose (inspiring creativity in children) but also produces a product that is a net negative for the planet (plastic bricks). The company recognises that they have fallen short in this area and are now exploring alternative materials that will allow them to meet their net zero goal.

For us, therefore, LEGO is a clear example of a BBOP. Its leaders are seeking to balance their business goals with their societal ones and taking action to address any issues that stand in their way. They may not be perfect, but they're choosing to head in the right direction.

Deliberately, on purpose

It's worth noting up front that there are two dimensions to our concept of 'on purpose'. The first is the meaningful impact you're seeking to deliver; the second is the deliberate approach you're taking to do so.

BBOP leaders do both, actively choosing to operate in a purposeful way. When this is done well, everything else falls into place.

Want to become a BBOP?

Interested? Want to know how your business can become a BBOP? It won't just happen overnight. It will take effort, diligence and application.

In this book, we will show you how.

SECTION 1

SHIFTS IN THINKING

Introduction

In 1963, the Milton Bradley Company copyrighted the board game *The Game of Life,* which had been around in one form or another for over 100 years.

As the name suggests, it takes players on a lifetime journey, with the aim of building up as much wealth as possible. The winner is the one who hits millionaire status and gets to retire in style. Losers are designated bankrupt, forced to retire to the country and become philosophers.

For children, it's great fun; a brightly coloured board game with a spinning wheel and cars as counters. But as adults, with the benefit of experience, it feels like a symbol of how things have all gone a bit wrong.

Modern capitalism instils a set of behaviours that encourage us to optimise for wealth rather than optimising for life. It's the way we're encouraged to think, and the way that businesses are rated and measured. This explains why so many people end up chasing money at the cost of so much more.

Why we need to hack our brains

For those of us who believe there's a better way to work, the first step is to shift the way we think. To roll back these behaviours and values, which we have learned from a young age, and replace them with better, more compassionate approaches that seek more than financial fulfilment. In short, to build a Better Business On Purpose.

However, while we may have been able to develop opposable thumbs, evolution has left us unprepared in the '*on purpose'* department. So if we're going to become agile changemakers, we need to hack our brains, shift our thinking and overcome our embedded behaviours.

And that means understanding what these behaviours are – and what better alternatives might look like.

Here's a whizz through the principles and practices that we need to push back against:

Financial maximisation

A widespread belief which sets an expectation that, in any decision, the right choice is the one that makes the most money, regardless of other factors.

Winner takes all

A zero-sum game, in which winners get ahead at the expense of losers. The effect of this is that the rich get richer and leave the rest behind.

Playing to win

The combination of our competitive instinct and societal norms means we're fearful of rivals, and pre-set to compete, rather than to find ways to support, share and collaborate.

Outworking the competition

The acceptance that, in the economic balance of cost vs time vs quality, time (and the person who spends it) is most likely to be deprioritised.

Incentivisation of short-term gains

Financial maximisation tends to trigger short-term financial targets and incentive structures, which encourage people to do things they don't believe in, at the expense of sustainable growth.

Growth for growth's sake

Focusing only on profit can blind us to the wider costs of growth. It drives consumerism, leading to people buying things they don't need, as well as to underpaid workers, planned obsolescence and more landfill.

Sweating the assets
Optimising for financial maximisation creates an environment in which everything, and everyone, becomes an asset to be worked as hard as possible, for the benefit of the bottom line.

Leading by head not heart
Basing business models on financial spreadsheets means emotional considerations can get lost or, worse still, dismissed.

The impact of shifting our thinking

The tricky thing is, we're all infected with a hidden default bias. We save effort by sticking with the behaviours we've learned, even when there's a better way.

But when business leaders do this, the impact can be massively negative. It leads to a lack of long-term vision or investment, and to people and customers being treated as numbers. It leads to faceless organisations which knowingly do more harm than good, doing deals where one side loses so that the other side can win. It even leads to the existence of the Japanese word *karoshi*, which means *overwork death* (and is such a stark contrast to the beautiful Norwegian word *arbeidsglede*, meaning *joy at work*).

All of which, eventually, leads to the development of huge companies like Google, which started out with a clear and simple purpose and intention, *'Don't be evil'*, and, it is argued, then relegated it once they'd reached a monopolistic scale. If you're not careful, it could lead to your business looking just like all the others, and lacking soul.

But just imagine, for a minute, what would have happened if Google had held onto that mantra? What if they had chosen to move away from learned behaviours and build a Better Business On Purpose?

In the following chapters, we'll take you through the shifts in thinking that will help you do just that.

OVER TO YOU...

The best decision isn't the one that maximises wealth for a few lucky people at the top, or that ignores the impact to people's lives, local communities and the planet. Sounds obvious, perhaps, but only if we put financial maximisation back in its place.

Businesses which are guided by a clear purpose don't ignore the concept of profit; they need to make money to achieve their goals. But they balance it with other, equally important concepts and work hard to keep that balance right.

That's why it's so important not just to build a business, but to build a Better Business On Purpose. And to do that, we need to work against our in-built behaviours and start to shift the way we think. Are you in?

THE 9 SHIFTS THAT WILL TRANSFORM YOUR APPROACH TO BUSINESS

FROM → TO

1. VALUE → VALUES

2. UNICORNS → ZEBRAS

3. GLOBAL WEALTH GAP → EQUALITY REVOLUTION

4. STATE POWER → TECH POWER → PEOPLE POWER

5. TECH FEAR → TECH CONFIDENCE

6. COMMAND & CONTROL → ANYTIME, ANYWHERE

7. CLIMATE DISASTER → ECOLOGICAL RECOVERY

8. ME ME ME → THE GREATER GOOD

9. GLOBAL PANDEMIC → GLOBAL POSSIBILITY

Shift 1: From value to values

For too long, companies have based the way they operate on the sole priority of making money – seemingly at almost any cost. But change is on the way; businesses are evolving, with increasing numbers of founders and leaders seeing profit as a way to achieve their goals, not a goal in itself.

Why the Mullet Economy is (thankfully) out of fashion

Back in 1976, the economist and Nobel Prize winner Milton Friedman established the theory that the main responsibility of any business was to create as much money as possible for its shareholders. It was an infectious idea, and in the years since, companies across the globe have passed it on, creating a norm in which the tail (finance) wags the dog (corporate decision making).

This acceptance of Friedman's model has led to a Stepford-esque homogenisation of almost every aspect of life. From the high street and the shopping centre to the film, music and other creative industries, everything looks the same. While that's pretty dull on a day-to-day level, it's also a wider business and societal problem.

The focus on replicating what has worked before means that fewer risks are taken, and fresh business initiatives and creativity are side-lined in the pursuit of safely achievable profit. Would-be entrepreneurs struggle to create an audience for their brilliant new ideas against the might of global brands. Consumers are left with movie reboots and sequels, sound-a-like pop songs and identikit clothes.

But the good news is, the pushback has started. Yancey Strickler, co-founder of the Kickstarter crowdfunding platform, is among those calling it out.

In his inspirational book, *This Could Be Our Future*, Strickler described Friedman's theory as the Mullet Economy, because *'Like the hairstyle, it is business upfront and party in the back'*. His argument was that not only is Friedman's theory misguided, but also that it is becoming irrelevant, due to the way the world is changing.

There's evidence to suggest that our hair-metaphor-loving friend is right – and as we explain in more detail in Shift 8, the younger generation are leading the charge. Whilst it's important not to overgeneralise, it's well accepted that they are a more empathetic bunch than the old guard, and that they tend to look at a bigger picture which goes beyond the agenda of financial success at any cost.

In their view, it is no longer acceptable to cream off company profits at the expense of the customer, the employees on the shop floor and the environment. This has been reflected in, or has triggered, an era of conscious or liberal capitalism (as defined in 'Shifts in Doing; Purpose'), led by a growing number of radical business founders, who have chosen to do things differently and become a force for good. Step forward nature lover, activist, mountain climber and self-confessed dirtbag, Yvon Chouinard, founder of Patagonia[1].

"Profits happen when you do everything else right."

Chouinard's approach to business chimes perfectly with this prioritisation of values above value. In his excellently named book, *Let My People Go Surfing*[2], he explains how, after massive growth during the 70s and 80s, his chain of outdoor activity clothing stores hit a plateau. As thoughtful leaders do, he sought expert advice on where to take his business next.

However, when the answer came back that it was time for him to sell up and retire, Chouinard wasn't having any of it. He was still full of energy and ideas and didn't believe it was time to stop. His commitment to his employees, his customers and the environment was as strong and as passionate as it had ever been.

Never one to sit around and wait, Chouinard flew his leadership team to the real Patagonia in Argentina, for an emergency re-group. He worked with them to establish a new set of core values, which they adhere to, to this day.

Chief amongst these was the principle that *'All company decisions must be made in light of the environmental crisis... we must strive to do no harm'*, and that *'Without wishing to give its achievement primacy, we wish to profit on our activities. However, growth and expansion are values not basic to this corporation'*.

Patagonia have inevitably made mistakes along the way – but their values mean they recognise and learn from them. For example, having grasped the damage that even organic cotton production can do to the environment, they have changed the materials they use, for good.

Their agenda remains clear: as Chouinard notes,

> *'A company needs to be profitable in order to stay in business and accomplish all its other goals'* – not for profit itself.

He is a living example of BBOP, proving that it is possible to generate profit alongside other ethical agendas. Thirty-odd years after he refocused his business, his company continues to fund activists and drive environmental change.

In 2022, Chouinard moved the ownership of the Patagonia company (worth around $3bn) to the Patagonia Purpose Trust and Holdfast Collective, a non-profit organisation with the purpose of making company profits (c. $100m per annum) available to combat the planet's ongoing climate catastrophe.

It was said that 'he literally gave his company to Mother Earth', and in doing so, he moved the goalposts for business leaders the world over, redefining once more what it means for a business to truly be a force for good.

OVER TO YOU...

Profit in and of itself is no bad thing. It gives you the opportunity to be even more purpose-led, to encourage creativity and explore new ways of doing business, such as investing in environmentally sound materials or providing a company crèche.

The problem comes when businesses put profit at the expense of people and the planet, which is not only morally questionable, but also environmentally unsustainable.

A business which is purpose-driven and profit-making is the best of all worlds. Is that your approach? If not, could it be?

BBOP in action: TOMS Shoes

In 2006, while on holiday in Argentina, Blake Mycoskie met a volunteer who was delivering shoes to children. After offering to help her, he was struck by the sheer number of shoeless children that he met, and was inspired to start a business, TOMS Shoes, which provided a solution as well as a product.

Mycoskie's founding principle was the One for One® model, through which the company gives a free pair of shoes to a child in need for every pair they sell. In the intervening years, the company has donated 100,000,000 pairs of shoes, positively impacting millions of lives, and now commits one third of its profits to grassroot activities.

Daniel H. Pink, best-selling author and chief speech writer for former US Vice President Al Gore, has described TOMS Shoes' business model as *'Expressly built for **purpose** maximisation.'*

We couldn't have put it better ourselves.

"If we're going to become agile changemakers, we need to hack our brains, shift our thinking and overcome our embedded behaviours."

Nikki Gatenby

Shift 2: From unicorns to zebras

Value is a changeable beast. Commercial principles which are fully accepted by one generation can be shed like a skin by the next, as each one seeks to re-evaluate what matters and question what value actually means. Increasingly – and positively – this is leading people to challenge the legitimacy of companies which glorify the pursuit of profit, above all else.

The dangerous fantasy of unicorn businesses

Do unicorns exist? In the business world they do; they're defined as privately held start-up companies which are valued at $1bn or more. Silicon Valley has been chasing these kinds of companies for years, and investors seek to throw money at them, in the hope of magical results.

Unfortunately, just like their animal equivalents, the majority of them are enticing, insubstantial, and rooted in fantasy. And the profits they promise are all too often an illusion.

Take WeWork[3], a company created by Adam Neumann, with the initial good intention of providing flexible premises for start-ups. Neumann raised $1.7bn in private capital, and the company was valued at $16bn in 2016, despite having never turned a profit. By 2019, following a failed IPO, the reported valuation of the company had fallen by 89%, and its people were left to fend for themselves.

As Rebecca Honeyman, co-founder of SourceCode Communications, noted in *TechCrunch*, instead of WeWork being a successful unicorn, *'It was really a one-trick pony with a cardboard horn.'*

More recently, in the run-up to its IPO in March 2021, Deliveroo was valued at £8.8bn by Goldman Sachs and J.P. Morgan. They appeared to think that the £224m loss the company made in 2020 was negated by the pandemic-fuelled boost in fast-food takeaway deliveries; but the market wasn't fooled. Deliveroo was called out on significant ESG (environmental, social and governance) sustainability issues, and its share price fell by over 30% on the first day of trading.[4]

The IPO was described as *'A dog's dinner'* and *'A case study of how not to do an IPO'* by Fraser Thorne, CEO of the Edison Group. And the gig-economy model on which it was based has been described as *'A race to the bottom, with employees in the main treated as disposable assets – which is the very antithesis of a sustainable business model'* by Eden Tree Investment Management.

Enter the zebra, the real-life business beast

The good news is, there is another way to grow companies, which doesn't involve raising enormous amounts of equity for a potential pipe dream. And in a neat zoological twist, the companies that work in this way are known as zebras[5].

Unlike unicorns, zebras are real, and their business equivalents are based in reality too (always helpful). They do real business, rather than simply disrupting existing markets, or piggybacking on existing resources, or pushing their agenda so hard that rules begin to bend, and people start to break (we're looking at you, Uber).

Zebra companies tend to be led by experts in their fields, who are able to monetise their passion because of their level of understanding of their market and customers. Yes, they achieve profit, but they also create positive impact. And they do so in a sustainable way, over time, rather than building an illusion that others will fund.

They also tend to have social goals, seeking to fix or solve a societal problem, and be a force for good in the world. And they are two-tone, for-profit and for their cause. Like TomboyX, creators of unisex underwear designed to fit who their customers are, not who they are told to aspire to be. Their hero product is boxer briefs for women – created by popular demand, produced sustainably, delivering against the bottom line as well as against the company's ethos. A zebra in all but name.

The jeans-based zebra that reclaimed a town's soul

There's a little-known town in Wales called Cardigan which, ironically, was home to a jeans factory for 40 years. It produced 35,000 pairs of jeans each week, until the factory was closed in 2002 in an effort to cut costs. Four hundred people lost their jobs, and the town lost a little bit of its soul.

Then in came Clare and David Hieatt, who had sold their previous sustainable clothing brand, Howies, to US firm Timberland. They took on a factory and set up the Hiut Denim Company, aiming to recreate the 400 lost jobs, use the skill on their doorstep and breathe new life into their community. Their philosophy is *'Do one thing well'* and they're certainly succeeding; Hiut Denim Company is now a globally recognised brand.

But this success hasn't been achieved by a headline-generating IPO or a clampdown on employee rights. Clare and David are following the way of the zebra, growing steadily by making 200 pairs of jeans every week.

They're not falling into the trap of overcommitting, despite the global demand; instead, they're choosing to honour and respect the *'grand masters'* behind the sewing machines, creating sustainable jeans with free repairs. For life.

OVER TO YOU...

Unlike their unicorn counterparts, zebra companies are lean, efficient and consistent. They value people more than media headlines and seek profit for social good, rather than for glory, sustainably funding their positive impact on the world. A world which would be a better place if people ignored the shallow appeal of the unicorns and instead threw their efforts into creating more zebras.[6]

So how do you fit into this metaphorical zoo? Are you making a conscious effort to build a sustainable business, or chasing a financial fantasy?

BBOP in action: Tony's Chocolonely

There's a dark secret at the heart of most chocolate production that leaves a particularly nasty taste in the mouth. Dutch journalist Teun van de Keuken has made it his business to bring it into the light – and offer an alternative.

In 2003, having uncovered the extent of illegal child labour and modern slavery throughout the chocolate supply chain, van de Keuken set out to raise awareness of the problem, and shame international chocolate makers into action. So he ate a pile of chocolate bars on a Dutch TV show and turned himself in as a chocolate criminal to the Dutch authorities.

No one, not even the manufacturers, took him seriously. So he took matters into his own hands and launched Tony's Chocolonely, the world's first *'100% slave-free'* chocolate bar, in 2005.

By the end of 2018, Tony's Chocolonely had become the No. 1 chocolate brand in the Netherlands, selling more than multinationals Verkade, Mars and Nestlé. And although this growth is seriously impressive, that's not the point.

As noted in *Forbes* magazine[7], Tony's Chocolonely is *'An impact company, that happens to make chocolate.'* The company's mission isn't just to create one slave-free chocolate bar, or even one slave-free brand, but to inspire the industry to make all chocolate on that basis.

This enabled the founders to raise funding from investors who shared their ethical ideals and were happy for them to retain majority voting rights, as well as to put 15% of company shares in employees' hands.

This zebra isn't about wealth creation, or making great chocolate. It's what zebras are all about: business as a force for good. And when that happens, the stars align and the unicorns retreat.

Shift 3: From global wealth gap to equality revolution

Global wealth inequality is rife. From zillionaire CEOs to family money aristocrats, the rich are getting richer, and the gap between them and the rest of the world is widening.

And while there's a growing sense that the issue needs tackling, it's not yet translated into the social and corporate rethink that will trigger large scale change. What will it take to readdress the balance, and how can being a Better Business On Purpose help?

Closing the gap between the haves and have-nots

We're all aware of the wealth gap that exists today, but it's easy to underestimate just how ridiculously massive it is. So let's break it down:

Combined wealth of the richest eight people on the planet:	£350 billion
Combined wealth of the poorest 3.5 billion people on the planet:	£350 billion

Yep, you read that right (and it may have made you feel more than a little nauseous). Just eight people have as much financial wealth as half the world's population. In the time it will take you to read this paragraph, one of the wealthiest of them all, Amazon founder and CEO Jeff Bezos, will have made the annual salary of his lowest paid employee. $30,000 in just 11.5 seconds. That's not a wealth gap, it's a chasm.

Inequality is as old as society itself, but it seems to be becoming more extreme. In 1960, a CEO typically earned 20 times as much as the median employee. Today it's more like 354 times and in some companies it's higher still; for Ocado, a UK online supermarket, the CEO/median employee ratio is an eyewatering 2,605:1.

Undervaluing those who add value

To be fair, most CEOs and founders work really hard. But that shouldn't equate to them being worth so much more than the rest of us.

During the pandemic, many of us in the UK stood outside our homes on Thursday evenings and clapped our respect for frontline NHS staff. However, it would take an NHS nurse more than 17 lifetimes to earn as much as the highest-paid UK hedge fund manager earns in a year (£31 million).

No one claps for the hedge fund managers; on that kind of salary, they probably don't care. But it can't be right that they are so highly valued compared to people for whom saving lives is just the day job. These ridiculous levels of inequality seem to be accepted as just the way things are. Why are we not more outraged?

Could reworking the four horsemen trigger an inequality apocalypse?

History has shown that the best ways to significantly reduce runaway inequality are disease and destruction. And in his book, *The Great Leveler: Violence and the History of Inequality from the Stone Age to the Twenty-First Century,* Stanford's Professor Walter Scheidel identifies four 'horsemen' for today's world that could trigger a 21st century, inequality-banishing apocalypse.

In order of terrifyingness, they are war, deadly pandemics, state collapse and revolution. None of them sound like fun ways to achieve this goal... but they're worth exploring nonetheless:

War

War reduces inequality because lots of people die, leading to a reset and a natural redistribution of wealth. This is the most extreme of Scheidel's four horsemen, and not something we'd advocate pursuing.

Deadly pandemics

The pandemics that Scheidel refers to include the medieval-era Black Death, which killed a third of Europe's population, and the 1918 Spanish Flu, which wiped out a third of the world's population. Both of which led to a massive shortage of available labour and, in turn, a smaller income gap.

In comparison, Covid-19 confirmed deaths at the time of writing account for less than 0.001% of the world's population. This is due to a range of factors including the ability to coordinate lockdowns and the speedy development of vaccines, both supported by technology that didn't exist in 1918.

So future pandemics are unlikely to reduce inequality in the same way. Indeed, the Covid-19 pandemic of 2020 has so far had the opposite effect. As Dan Price (company founder) explains:

> *'Workers around the world lost $3.7 trillion in the pandemic. Billionaires around the world gained $3.9 trillion in the pandemic. It's the biggest one-year wealth transfer in history, yet somehow barely anyone is talking about it.'*

State collapse

Scheidel's view on state collapse is that it lessens inequality by putting power into the hands of the previously disenfranchised. Once again, it's an extreme way to proceed, and one that we're not ready to champion.

However, it certainly seems a reasonable assumption that, as power shifts from states to tech to people (as explored in Shift 4), people could become more equal as a result.

Revolution

Finally, Scheidel notes the way that a revolution turns the status quo on its head, leading to a reduction (or at least a change) in levels of inequality. And this feels like a catalyst for change we can really get behind. We're not talking pitchforks and guillotines, but a different kind of revolution, in which the speed and scale of technological developments trigger global changes.

Take the rapid rise of crypto currencies as an alternative, decentralised store of value (again, something we explore in Shift 4). Then take it a step further, with the advent of DeFi (short for decentralised finance), a completely alternative banking system which replaces the need for banks and intermediaries like Visa and PayPal.

Could we see a technological revolution, that triggers global changes to inequality in the way that traditional revolutions have done? And if so, what would the role of BBOP be?

The uptake in Certified B Corporation businesses provides a clue and demonstrates the role that BBOP can play in driving value beyond shareholders alone. As part of the accreditation process, B Corps are required to include a commitment in their Articles of Association to *'promote the success of the company for the benefit of its members and, through its business and operations, to have a material positive impact on society and the environment, taken as a whole'.*

Changing the fundamental legal structure of an organisation in a way that meets unjust inequality head on? That's a BBOP gamechanger that takes the principles behind self-imposed CEO wage cuts to a whole new level. One that, if it became the norm, could be the start of the kindest, most socially impactful revolution to date.

OVER TO YOU...

We're big fans of B Corporation accreditation, and the thinking behind it. We also recognise that in a business's early days, or during turbulent times, it could become a distraction from building a stable, sustainable and profitable business.

So if Certified B Corp status isn't right for you right now, what could you take from the principles it's built on? How could you structure your business to make it a force for good that meets unjust inequality head-on?

Shift 4: From state power to tech power to people power

Colonialism kicked off in Europe in the 15th century, a point in history which is now referred to as the Age of Capitalism. Colonies were established to control and assert power over people with the aim of economic dominance. And until recent times, global power has remained firmly with nation states.

But today a huge shift in power is playing out, away from nation states via technology businesses to the people. What can we learn from this? And should we be dismissive of these new power centres, or are they paving the way for a movement towards Better Business On Purpose?

How age-old norms around power have been turned on their heads

There's a mountain of evidence to suggest that globalisation, the internet and the rise of technology have shifted where influence lies. Here's one (pretty shocking) example.

In August 2019, when Donald Trump was weighing up the implications of a trade war with China, he met with Apple CEO Tim Cook to discuss the potential impact on Apple's interests. No, we're not kidding; the president of the USA was so concerned about how his decision might affect a company that he invited its leader in for tea and a chat. This was unimaginable even 10 years before (though to be fair, Trump as POTUS was pretty unimaginable back then too).

But now here we are, in a world where a handful of tech companies have come from nowhere to become global powerhouses.

"Things were created to be used. The reason why the world is in chaos is because things are being loved and people are being used."

The Dalai Lama

These organisations, known by the initialism FAAMG (standing for Facebook/Meta, Apple, Amazon, Microsoft and Google) are the five biggest tech companies of our time. They're money-making machines, accumulating wealth at an incredible rate; at the time of writing, they have a combined value of $7.6 trillion, which ranks the group as the third biggest 'country' in the world (by GDP).

FAAMG operate globally, rising above any single jurisdiction, with growing power. They are pushing the rules to the limit or finding ways around them. Despite G7 discussions around global taxation, they seem to be getting away with it, further fuelling the shift of power away from nation states.

How the FAAMG power grab evolved

Now, none of this happened by accident, or because their founders were geniuses (though they are, let's be fair, pretty smart). FAAMG and other tech giants have been able to scale at speed due to some ultra-recent developments unique to software industries:

→ Abundant, affordable(ish) electricity in most developed nations.

→ High-speed, always-on internet, widely available.

→ Open source technologies (generally developed for free by passionate IT engineers), such as web servers, email, and internet messaging protocols and standards (such as http and www).

→ The cloud – a slightly confusing name for simplifying the role of physical, networked servers, which makes it easy to securely scale your software to everyone in the world at once.

→ Smart phones – which are basically a computer in your pocket, packed with features you want to use, and platforms accessible by a single app, making it easier to reach more people.

What this means is that tech businesses have an inherent advantage when it comes to scaling what they do, compared to traditional companies.

To pick a real-life example, a steel beam manufacturer has to grapple with manufacturing, labour, storage and distribution costs for each beam it produces. Whereas, with a software product, once the first one is made, it's possible to recreate millions or even billions of them (in an instant, for relatively little cost, and with a ridiculously high margin), and deliver them to customers with the click of a button.

Next up: people power fuelled by technology?

Whatever your view of FAAMG, they clearly illustrate how power is shifting. Yes, they are money-making machines, with an interesting relationship with tax accountability. Yes, they are typically ubiquitous, with a history of competition crushing and market monopolisation and yes, some of the purpose-fuelled intentions they started out with appear to have got lost along the way.

But FAAMG and other tech powerhouses are also breaking down borders and connecting people. They are challenging stale and confused politics and legislation at a global level. As a result, it could be argued, they are also leading a further shift – towards the democratisation of power.

Probably the best example of this right now is Bitcoin, which went from a value of $0 to $1 trillion in just 11 years (compared to 22 for Google and 44 for Microsoft). It's a completely decentralised technology with no corporate structure; no one is in control, and no one can take control. It works across borders and is open source; technically, anyone who can be bothered can explore how it works, and try to improve it.

Additionally, Bitcoin's creator is anonymous, going by the pseudonym Satoshi Nakamoto. So there's no fame or ego at play here. At its core, cryptocurrency is technology created with the purpose of using technical innovation to reinvent a fairer, truly decentralised, global money system.

Technology plus purpose has the potential to transform society

Bitcoin shows us that power can become decentralised, and that purpose massively accelerates global change and adoption. This readiness to adopt new things is already the norm for the next generation.

To give just one example, the hot-ticket Christmas present for young teens in 2020 was Robux. Not a robot, or any kind of physical toy, but a digital currency that they could spend on cool virtual things like sneakers, islands and swords, to impress their friends while playing an online game called Roblox.

Put all this together, and who knows what incredible and life-changing concepts may be around the corner?

Take the history of medicine, a life-or-death example of the impact and rapid speed of change. For thousands of years, if you scratched your finger, there was a reasonable chance it would become infected, and you could die. In just a few decades, the arrival of antiseptic meant that a scratch was just a scratch.

This sort of exponential change is happening again today and, like the introduction of antiseptic, the outcome may well be something to embrace rather than to fear.

It offers an opportunity for BBOP founders, who now have the ability to create businesses that are a force for good in the world, positively impacting billions of people, even with limited resources.

So we may, if we're lucky, be on the brink of a world where power is decentralised and borderless, bringing people and purpose together: where new, fairer forms of money replace monetary systems that are linked to the state, and where power structures that exist to maximise shareholder value are overturned by better businesses on purpose.

Meanwhile, governments around the world are trying their best to navigate the rapid onset of Web3 innovation (starting with the decentralisation of the web based on blockchain) and define their role within these new markets.

To use another example from the medical world, whilst Professor Sarah Gilbert was developing the Oxford AstraZeneca vaccine, based on double stranded DNA (see Shift 9), Dr Kati Kariko was working in parallel on the single strand mRNA that was the foundation to both Pfizer-Biontech and Moderna vaccines.

An unassuming biotech researcher, Dr Kariko[8] has said that her dream was to *'develop something in the lab that helps people'*, not for the money, but for the impact. Building on layers and layers of academic breakthroughs, she has taken a novel approach to mRNA, a method devised to instruct cells to make their own medicines, including vaccines.

At the time of writing, this ground-breaking technical development has led to COVID vaccinations around the world, and may lead to new treatments for previously incurable diseases. None of which would have happened without the brilliant combination of purpose and an enforced democratisation of power, away from big money and towards socially minded academics.

OVER TO YOU...

The global shift in power, from nation states, to businesses, to people, looks set to continue. And while true democracy at scale is hard to police, it's undeniable that technology is overhauling traditional, state-led norms.

For those of us who are purpose-led, there's never been a better time to start a company with the intent to change the world for the better. What part will your business play in this power shift?

"History doesn't repeat itself, but it often rhymes."

Mark Twain

FAAMG: How it started... how it's going

It's fair to say that the FAAMG companies' founding intentions and present realities don't really align. Here's a reminder of how three of these fast-growing, dominant tech brands started out.

Google

Set out with the intention to *'organise the world's information'* (underpinned by the instruction *'Don't be evil'*). Their timing was perfect, and they went on to deliver; by 2002, they'd made the content labyrinth that is the internet searchable at lightning speed. They followed up with an impressive project to scan and digitise the world's book collection, succeeding with 25 million university books before copyright issues scuppered their plans.

Microsoft

Launched with the honourable mission to *'put a computer on every desk'*. Founder Bill Gates could see the potential that the computer had to offer, and he and his friend Paul Allen set out to provide it to the masses. Little did they know that desks were just the beginning, as technology carried them into the world of laps and pockets.

Amazon

Jeff Bezos started Amazon with the intention of being *'Earth's most customer-centric company, where customers can find and discover anything they might want to buy online, and which endeavours to offer its customers the lowest possible prices'*. They began with books, and used technology to reinvent end-to-end supply chains, highlighting the potential of e-commerce.

It could be argued, then, that these companies started out as BBOPs. Their original intentions were driven by a clear sense of purpose and their early employees were super engaged, because the journey they were on was so exciting, and so meaningful.

BBOP in action: The people versus the ESL

In 2021, the Spanish billionaire and president of Real Madrid, Florentino Pérez, spearheaded a project to create a European Super League.

Pérez and a cohort of other wealthy benefactors had come up with what they thought was a brilliant plan: to create a new football league which would guarantee 15 permanent 'founding' places for Europe's elite (i.e. richest) teams, and five others for which teams could qualify each year. Once the founders were in, they were in forever, however appallingly they might subsequently play.

However, while this may have seemed like a smashing idea to the billionaire owners and their friends, the players, managers, commentators and fans saw things differently. They shared an overwhelming view that the ESL was contrary to the spirit of football and the ability of underdogs to surpass expectations. They believed that the game belonged to them – and they weren't about to give it up.

As soon as the European Super League was formally announced, people spoke up and took action, flooding social media with criticism of the plans. Within minutes, the story was everywhere; within just 48 hours, the project had collapsed. The money-men lost, and the fans won.

On a wider scale, society won, as the trouncing of the ESL was a triumph for the democratisation of power, and the passion and shared purpose of the masses.

However, the bigger you get, the harder it is to stay true to your ideals. So if you don't make a deliberate decision to remain a force for good, the focus on making money can overpower the desire to create impact.

FAAMG may not have intended to become highly criticised global money machines, but many would argue that, as a result of this imbalance, that's where they've ended up.

Shift 5: From tech fear to tech confidence

The huge role that technology now plays in our lives can be seen as a blessing, a curse or a challenge – or all three, at once. But while some fear the speed of innovation in general, and the growth of artificial intelligence (AI) in particular, it's our belief that the balance is in our favour, and that innovation is changing the quality of our lives and businesses for the better.

By deciding to embrace and engage with this change, especially where technology helps us to optimise our operations, we will be better placed to create better businesses on purpose.

Busting the myths about the growth of technology

For those of us who grew up in the 70s and 80s, and especially those who were glued to *Tomorrow's World*, technology was billed as the answer to all society's problems. As computers got more sophisticated, the prediction went, tasks would become easier and more efficient, or disappear entirely, freeing us up for a life of leisure.

Fast forward 30 years or so, and some hold the opposite view, captured in cultural icons such as the *Terminator* movies and TV's *Black Mirror,* that technology and the AI it enables are growing unstoppably, and out to get us. Who's right?

We'd argue that technological innovation, fuelled by the international exchange of ideas, is actually having a hugely positive impact on society; and that the wilder predictions rarely materialise. Here are some techno-myths that have been well and truly busted.

"All jobs are under threat from robots"

While it's true that some jobs are being replaced by technology, research from PWC[9] has predicted that on balance, for each job lost as a result of the application of AI, a new one is created in a different sector or industry. Furthermore, the jobs that we're losing seem to be ones we're unlikely to miss; known, if you'll excuse the asterisk, as bullsh*t jobs.

A great example of this is the use of AI in recognising car number plates. It's not a thrilling job, nor one that needs a person. Using technology to carry it out frees up people to be engaged in something more rewarding and worthwhile.

Now clearly, some groups of workers are particularly vulnerable to advances in tech. For example, many supermarket checkout operators are facing redundancy and may need support to reskill; and as a society, we have a responsibility to ensure they are presented with new opportunities.

But for the foreseeable future, AI systems will be unable to think for themselves, leaving jobs involving conscious human thought, moral decision-making or original creative thinking to us humans.[10]

"Technology moves so fast that we can't cope with the change"

So often, when a new piece of technology or scientific development is announced, it's assumed that massive advances will follow at a dizzying pace. In reality, these things take time.

The first driverless car was built by Norman Bel Geddes and shown at the 1939 General Motors exhibition. More than 80 years later, they are hardly overrunning the streets.

This is partly because of concerns around their ability to make decisions in life-and-death situations, and partly because no insurance company has effectively tackled the risk probabilities. It's also not helped by the fact that people are still a little bit scared to trust a robot (despite human error being a factor in 95% of all road accidents – a factor which disappears when AI is in the driving seat).

Like the hoverboard, the jet pack and intergalactic space travel, the rate of adoption of driverless cars has hardly been too fast for us to handle.

"Big technological developments come with big risks"

There have been many warnings about tech-based destruction, such as a malfunctioning of the nuclear codes triggering nuclear war, or the millennium bug causing a global meltdown. Thankfully, despite the acres of news coverage and heralding of doom, actual catastrophes are rare.

Why? Because when scientists (or journalists) make these kinds of predictions, they don't know what they don't know. Back in 1894, for example, *The Times* newspaper predicted that every street in London would be buried under nine feet of manure by 1950, such was the frequency at which horse-drawn vehicles were being used in the city. While that might have made sense based on the facts available to them at the time, it failed to take into account the invention of the petrol engine and the car.

When negative predictions about technological developments do come true, it's usually because of specific, unusual circumstances, and rarely within the predicted timeframes. More often than not, they happen not with a bang, but a whimper.

The flipside of technology: an endless cycle of improvement

Underpinning these dystopian predictions about how technology is destroying our futures is the argument that *'Things used to be better in the old days'*. Clearly not all change is good, but a glance at the big picture shows that human lives have improved immeasurably over time.

Unlike any other species on this planet, humans have both the ability and the desire to learn – from our peers, or from other resources – and to pass that learning on. As a result, we live in a world of infinite possibility, driven by the human passion for discovery. A world in which ideas, for the large part, are freely exchanged, fuel innovation and make stagnation near impossible.

As little as 300 years ago, humans had to spend the majority of their time hunting, foraging, farming and collecting water and wood, just to live. Today, thanks to human-driven innovation, our food is available from shops or online, utility companies pipe their resources to our properties, and products like computers and washing machines take much of the grunt work away.

These domestic changes alone have freed up huge amounts of time for us to work on what we choose, and to think creatively. And on a wider scale, the sharing of ideas, and humanity's natural desire to troubleshoot problems, have led us to develop life-improving technological solutions.

To pick just one example; it seems hard to imagine now, but as recently as the 1990s, the UK's Prime Minister, Tony Blair, was able to run the country without a mobile phone. By 2020, the ubiquity of smartphones led to the conviction of Minneapolis police officer Derek Chauvin, whose unlawful killing of George Floyd was filmed by a passer-by.

From the incredible advancements in medical science to the super-useful Google Maps app; from electric cars and renewable energy to online banking and software as a service products (aka SaaS); by any measure, it seems clear that the pluses of technology far outweigh the minuses. So instead of seeing technology as something to fear, we'd all be better off embracing its potential.

OVER TO YOU...

Clever technology, cleverly used, should be at the heart of building a Better Business On Purpose. As we look to future-proof our organisations, we should actively seek out the most relevant digital platforms and use AI and other software to apply them at scale, in a way that delivers positive impact.

At the same time, we should make sure we invest in our teams, enabling our people to succeed in roles which rely on creative thinking and empathy, and have purpose baked in.

As a business founder, how will you ensure that your workplace supports employees to combine the best bits of technology with the freedom to be creative, and thrive as a result?

Shift 6: From command and control to anytime, anywhere

One of the most vivid examples of how technology can change everyday life has been the explosion in remote working in the wake of the pandemic. This is just the latest in a series of significant shifts in the way that workplaces operate, with the power changing hands as we evolve. Over time, the balance between control and freedom is moving in the right direction... but there's more to be done.

How technology (and a pandemic) are turbo-charging the evolution of work

We spend around a third of our lives at work, but too few of us are enjoying it. Survey after survey has shown that employees are not happy in their jobs; one piece of data from the global Gallup survey suggests only 30% of people are engaged in the work that they do. By implication, the other 70% are just turning up and hoping to make it through the day without getting fired.

So how did we get here? And how can we escape?

Frederic Laloux, author of *Reinventing Organisations*, has mapped out the historical evolution of management thinking, in line with the stages of human development. He believes that going back to look at how workplace norms have evolved will help us find a positive, inclusive way forward.

Laloux's colour-coded concept plots out the journey from command-and-control organisations, such as the Mafia, via competition and growth-driven businesses like investment banks, to more idealistic, human-centred set-ups, guided by the pursuit of autonomy.

→ **RED** organisation – The Mafia, whose guiding metaphor is the 'Wolf Pack', with power exercised from the top.

→ **AMBER** organisation – Military, Religious and Government, whose guiding metaphor is 'Army', with highly formal, hierarchical roles.

→ **ORANGE** organisation – Multinational companies, investment banks, schools, whose guiding metaphor is 'Machine', where the goal is to beat the competition.

→ **GREEN** organisations – Businesses known for idealistic practices (Ben & Jerry's, Zappos), whose guiding metaphor is 'Family', with a focus on culture and empowerment.

→ **TEAL** organisation – Pioneers in new practice to thrive, whose guiding metaphor is 'Living Organism', driven by self-management and continual evolution.

Unfortunately, although very few businesses are now run according to the Mafia playbook (phew), there are equally few that have hit Team Teal (though you can read about one that is nailing the concept, Buurtzorg, in 'Shifts in Doing: People').

Too many are still operating under Laloux's red, amber and orange dynamics, sticking to the old-school ways of doing business. When instead they could be building on advances in management thinking, and global developments in technology, to create brilliant places to work.

How a global pandemic triggered exponential change

At the turn of the century, there was no Facebook, no Twitter, no YouTube. The iPhone was seven years away, and Zoom 11 years. Hard to believe, but true.

The massive developments in technology in the intervening years have led to an equally massive disruption to the status quo. WikiLeaks, fake news, the sharing economy, the gig economy, the rise of the unicorn company and the growth in AI... it's a whole new landscape.

But, as Mark Stevenson, an entrepreneur, author, broadcaster and expert on global trends, has noted, *'Technology is accelerating five times faster than management'.* The world around us has changed, but until very recently, many businesses, and business leaders, had failed to change to match.

And then in 2020, Covid-19 happened; and working norms changed almost overnight.

The word *unprecedented* has been overused to the point of destruction since the spring of 2020, but it's impossible to underestimate the impact of the pandemic on working practices.

In the preceding years, a degree of remote working was slowly becoming more acceptable. Global companies including Unilever, Twitter and Google had adopted a more flexible approach, supporting more employees to get the right balance between their work and lives.

But there were still a huge number of prevailing myths about working from home; for example, that it's bad for productivity, or that you can't trust your employees to work out of sight. Myths that were busted in a matter of days, as the world went into lockdown, and whole companies packed up and worked from home.

The new normal – and why there's (hopefully) no going back

Of course, not everyone got to stay at home during Covid-19. An army of fantastic key workers took care of us all, and kept the nation's wheels turning, by going into work.

But for office workers, the pandemic-forced experiment in flexible working turned everything on its head; according to *Forbes*, we saw a decade's worth of dramatic changes compressed into a single year. Thanks to platforms like Microsoft Teams, Zoom and Google Hangouts, people swapped exhausting commutes and face-to-face meetings for home-based, screen-based working. And in the new, virtual office, with more autonomy about how to manage the working day, many of us thrived.

More than two years on (at the time of writing) and there's not a huge appetite for the old normal. In May 2021, 43 of the UK's largest 50 employers said they were not planning to bring their staff back to the office full-time. The majority are embracing a mix of working from home, the office and elsewhere (known as hybrid working), which looks set to continue.

There are challenges within the hybrid model too, of course; work creep, employee isolation and the complexities involved in managing remote teams are all issues that leaders need to be aware of. And developing ludicrously good communication processes, and finding ways to bring people together for creativity and collaboration, will be critical too.

But it's fair to say that the new normal, and the autonomy it brings, is liberating for many. Indeed, future generations may struggle to believe that we once spent hours travelling by train to arrive at communal office buildings, only to put on headphones that drowned out our colleagues' chat, and wrap ourselves in blankets because the shared, germ-laden air conditioning was on full blast.

And as well as changing the way we work, Covid has made us question the way we think:

→   It has made us prioritise what we care about; health, wellbeing, safety, security and community. *Who we are* now matters more than *what we've got.*

→ It has made us reconsider how we value our real heroes, the frontline workers, who have had their capes hidden for far too long.

→ It has turned lives upside down, bringing into question why we do what we do, and whether it's worth it.

An unexpected outcome of this global period of reflection has been *'The Great Resignation'*, a term coined in response to Microsoft research which found that 41% of workers were considering quitting or changing their jobs in the wake of the pandemic.

So as the *anytime, anywhere* workplace continues to evolve, and more companies move through the colour chart to the heady heights of Team Teal, leaders also need to consider these questions, and build the answers into how they run their businesses.

OVER TO YOU...

As we emerge from the pandemic into the much-discussed future of work, we need to get clear on our priorities and make sure that the way we're managing our businesses, and our people, aligns with our determination to be a force for good.

We also need to develop workplace practices which enable our people to do their best work, and be their best selves. And we need to continue to keep up with the changes in technology that will make that possible.

Talented people have choices, so do you have a clear sense of purpose that your people can engage with? And do you have a compelling reason for people and clients to choose and stay with you? Right now, that's more important than ever.

"The future hasn't happened yet. The idea that our civilisation is doomed is not established fact. It is a story we tell ourselves."

John Higgs

Shift 7: From climate disaster to ecological recovery

Climate change is real. The impact of the human race on our planet has been unquestionably destructive. Yet, despite what you may have read, it is reversible.

As business leaders, we have a duty to do what we can to help avert the predicted disaster, and be a force for good on the ecological stage.

Will you join the growing number of companies that have made tackling the problem a core part of their purpose?

Ask not what your planet can do for you...

Aside from some high-octane celebrity deniers, its widely agreed that the human race is contributing to climate change. So far, so factual. But what's not quite so clear cut is whether the outlook is as bleak and irreversible as the media would have us believe.

Yes, there is irrefutable evidence of man-made ecological devastation across the world. Yes, we need to take global action to turn it around. But it *can* be turned around; environmental catastrophe is not inevitable. Unfortunately, we're being trained to think that it is.

Instead of rallying us around the cause, the apocalyptic way in which climate change is reported is having the opposite effect, prompting many to have an '*It's too late now... there's nothing I can do*' attitude. Others, faced with endless warnings of doom, are simply becoming immune.

Worse still, the more we hear about the impact that far-away governments and citizens are having on the planet – such as the catastrophic destruction of the Amazon rainforest – the easier it is to forget about similar problems on our doorstep. The overdevelopment of the UK, for example, has led to the decline of over half of UK species since the 1970s, including hedgehogs and turtle doves.

As John Higgs,[11] author of *The Future Starts Here*, writes: news such as this, in turn, feeds into a vicious circle in which *'the biggest cause of natural diversity loss is inaction through despair'*.

The impact of giving nature space to breathe

Far too rarely reported in the news is that, given the opportunity, nature thrives.

There are huge numbers of inspiring projects across the globe which are yielding spectacular results. Take rewilding, for example, which is defined as: *'Conservation efforts aimed at restoring and protecting natural processes and wilderness areas, often including the reintroduction of species of wild animals that have been driven out or exterminated.'*

Right now, thousands of landowners are exploring rewilding across the UK. Blazing a trail is the Knepp Estate in Sussex, whose rewilding project began all the way back in 2001. The results are astonishing; pop in for a visit and you'll meet reintroduced wild pigs, cattle, horses, storks and more.

Following in their footsteps is Roger Tempest, the current custodian of Broughton Hall in Yorkshire, who is working to reverse the adverse effects of centuries of farming on the land and wildlife. By the end of 2021, 450,000 trees will have been planted on the Broughton Estate, and a schedule of animal reintroductions is planned in the years ahead.

The sprawling estate was gifted to the Tempest family by William the Conqueror in the 1060s, and Roger and his colleague Kelly Hollick are taking a similarly long-term view, appreciating that work begun now will take years to come good, and will largely benefit future generations.

Tempest's actions are driven by a desire to champion a new way of life, and run a purpose-led business. For him, rewilding is part of a wider movement to live more meaningful lives, with deeper connections with nature. That is something we, as business leaders, can learn from.

Building businesses with a long-term view

In the face of adversity, the human race has a spectacular track record of problem-solving. Rewilding is just one of an increasing number of environmental initiatives that are beginning to reverse the damage we have collectively done to our planet.

While we're pretty sure that you won't find reintroducing wild animals included in many business strategies – not even those of BBOP champions – there's much that we can learn from Roger and his nature-loving contemporaries. We can take action to instigate change – sometimes dramatic, sometimes incremental – that will help diminish the impact of ecological destruction, even if it won't pay off for 5, 10 or even 50 years.

Think about oil- and plastic-eating fungi, sustainable energy, carbon-neutral beer companies and electric cars. At an individual level, consider John Pritchard, CEO of the inspirational Pala Eyewear brand.

Pritchard is dedicated to fighting poverty by transforming access to eye care in developing countries, including Burkina Faso, Zambia, Sierra Leone and Ethiopia.

Realising how life-changing clear sight can be, particularly in terms of earning an income, he set up Pala, a purpose-driven sunglasses company, which donates a proportion of its profits to VisionAid.

But Pala haven't stopped there. They discovered that they could re-use plastic as part of their sunglass case production in Africa, a win-win for all concerned. As Pritchard explains:

> 'For our sunglasses cases, we use manufacturing waste destined for landfill from a plastic- bag factory in Accra, as well as water sachets that have been simply discarded on the ground. The plastic is washed, cut and twisted into strands for weaving.

> 'Aside from being a better solution for the environment, the recycled plastic is proving to be an important solution for the communities, as the more traditional straw that has been used previously has become increasingly scarce due to climate change and the higher incidence of drought.'

Led by Pritchard, and driven by his purpose, Pala now has sustainability built into its supply chain and production, and continues to improve the employability and life-chances of people across the continent.

Some of these changes have immediate, transformational impact – in this case, seeing is literally believing. Others will take time to be fully realised.

But they're all proof, if we choose to see it, that in the face of ecological change, we're not as powerless as we might think.

OVER TO YOU...

As a business leader, you're in a position – and some might say, have the responsibility – to explore ways to minimise your environmental impact. And if you really want to make a difference, you should also adopt a more holistic approach, and work towards running a net-positive business.

How will you make sure that every step you take to do better business contributes to the global movement for good?

"We can work together to re-establish business as a force for good, and create better business, on purpose. We don't need to wait for the next pandemic; our work should begin now."

Nikki Gatenby

Shift 8: From me me me to the greater good

Contrary to the view that everything's going downhill, there's a real sense that we're living through a bit of a moment, in which self-centred consumerism is being replaced by collective responsibility. The fact that you're reading this book suggests that you're on board with the zeitgeist – so how will you bring it to life within your business?

The end of unconscious consumerism is nigh

Maybe we're optimists, maybe we're naive, but we (and many others) believe that the human race is on the brink of a new era.

One in which people and organisations will feel, and demonstrate, greater consideration for others and for themselves. In which Friedman's economic model, prioritising the pursuit of profit above all else, will take a back seat, and it will become second nature to consider the impact of our actions as part of our decision-making processes.

And while this movement towards the greater good was already gathering momentum before the pandemic, it's subsequently been turbo-charged, as lockdown gave us all the time and opportunity to reflect on our newfound quality of life, and question the global focus on consumerism, including shopping and travel.

This is a huge shift in both thinking and behaviour, underpinned by a simple principle: people care. They care about where the products they buy come from, and the ethics of the company that produced them. They care about the planet and its people, and how they're affected by globalisation and oppressive regimes.

They care about the growth of landfill, the loss of fish stocks, the erosion of indigenous culture.

And as a result, they care far less about having the latest clothes, or gadgets, or *stuff*.

How Generation Z is widening our collective lens

Aside from the pandemic, what's behind this growing emphasis on making things better all round? The changes that we've covered in previous shifts, such as developments in technology, and the need to tackle climate change, are all playing their part. But it's also got a lot to do with the collective mindset of Generation Z (those born between 1997 and 2012).

As ever, when it comes to discussing generational cohorts, it's important not to over-generalise. But there's evidence to suggest that Gen Z are the most coddled and monitored group in the history of our planet. And that all the nurturing and protecting has limited their exposure to challenge and adversity which, in turn, has led this generation to be more sensitive than their predecessors.

Now, it's fair to say that this sensitivity is a double-edged sword. There are concerns about the extent to which ill-thought-out social media posts can trigger an online lynch mob; and knee-jerk calls for people to be 'cancelled' based on historic actions make many of us uncomfortable. But at the same time, the way this generation care so much, about everything, is driving the movement towards a greater good.

The rise of empathetic economics

Certainly, the data suggests that the Gen Z lens is influencing how the majority of us view the world; a recent survey indicated that 90% of UK shoppers worry about the future of our planet. And this focus on ethical living is leading to a marked growth in ethical brands, and to people choosing to spend their money in line with their beliefs.

In 2020, for example, the biggest shift in consumer spending was for free-range eggs; it rose by 15.2%. Sales of plant-based products rose 11.4%, and sales of hybrid and electrical cars reached £5 billion for the first time. Online retailer Lyst noted a 47% increase in searches for 'organic cotton', 'vegan leather' and 'econyl', a regenerated nylon.

A third of shoppers now aim to buy more plant-based food and an equal number are actively seeking out Fairtrade goods. Over half intend to buy less single-use plastic, and 49% aim to become more energy efficient in the home. And the Co-op's December 2020 Ethical Consumerism Report claimed that UK ethical shopping exceeded £100bn in 2020, with further growth predicted year-on-year.

Today, then, materials matter, and shoppers care. And these changes in consumer attitudes and behaviour open up an opportunity for business leaders to reconsider how they operate, and bring their approach in line with the zeitgeist.

Writing in Forbes magazine, journalist Neil Parker set out his views on how these changes can, and should, directly impact the way that businesses sell their products. Here are some of his insights:

Consumers vs customers

Talking to people in their preferred way is a no-brainer for any business, and yet the word consume, which originally meant destroy by use or use up, is still the default. People who buy products and services would probably prefer to be referred to as shoppers, or customers.

Experience and access vs ownership

The backlash against stuff has led people to seek out experiences rather than own more things. When they do need something specific, they increasingly prefer to access it through a subscription or rental; worth considering within sales planning.

Customer knowledge vs the close

In a traditional sales pitch, everything leads to the close; the moment that you tip the customer into making a purchase. This is feeling increasingly old-school; today, a more relevant skill is to really understand the needs of your customers.

People expect your brand to not only provide solutions but to do so in a way that will enhance their lives. And if you can create a product that will genuinely make a difference to the world, the environment, or a community in need of support, they will love you for it.

Active vs passive customer care

Social media and the rise of online reviews have meant that the moment of purchase is no longer the end of the story. In just a few clicks, your products and customer service can be called out and ridiculed, or publicly championed; either way, the opinion is likely to be shared with hundreds of others.

What Parker really gets, and the rest of us must too, is that today's customer relationships are much more than just transactional; businesses need to provide their customers or clients with a full package of reasons to consider them. So building a Better Business On Purpose isn't just the right thing to do; it also makes sound business sense.

OVER TO YOU...

Infusing your business with a clear ethical conscience is a BBOP imperative. And while you may always have cared about doing the right thing, the way that people view the world today is making it a business decision as well as a personal one.

As we approach a new era of conscious-led choices, it's not just your product or service that customers will be interested in; your manifesto and agenda, the way you treat your employees, associates and partners, and your approach to the environment, will all shape how people perceive your business. How will you make sure they see you as you'd wish to be seen?

BBOP in action: Greta Thunberg

If there's one individual who represents the Gen Z triumph of care over consumerism, it's Greta Thunberg, the Swedish schoolgirl whose weekly *School strike for the climate* went from localised protest to global phenomenon, and became a rallying point for those who put planet over profit.

In April 2021, Thunberg's gamechanger credentials hit a new level when she appeared (virtually) at a US House Subcommittee, and called on Congress to enact more concrete measures on the climate disaster:[12]

> 'It is the year 2021. The fact that we are still having this discussion and even more that we are still subsidising fossil fuels directly or indirectly using taxpayer money is a disgrace...
>
> '...The gap between what we are doing and what actually needs to be done in order to stay below the 1.5 degrees Celsius target is widening by the second. And the simple and uncomfortable fact is that if we are to live up to our promises and commitments in the Paris Agreement, we have to end fossil fuel subsidies, stop new exploration and extraction, completely divest from fossil fuels and keep the carbon in the ground...
>
> '...And it may seem like we are asking for a lot, and you will of course say that we are naive, and that's fine. But at least we are not so naive that we believe things will be solved through countries and companies making vague and distant insufficient targets without any real pressure from the media and the general public.
>
> 'So either you do this, or you're going to have to explain to

your children and the most affected people, why you are surrendering on the 1.5 degree target. Giving up without even trying. What I am here to say is that unlike you, my generation will not give up without a fight...

'...How long do you honestly believe that people in power like you will get away with it? How long do you think you can continue to ignore the climate crisis, the global aspect of equity and historic emissions without being held accountable?

'You get away with it now, but sooner or later people are going to realise what you have been doing all this time, that's inevitable.

'You still have time to do the right thing and to save your legacies. But that window of time is not going to last for long. What happens then?

'We, the young people, are the ones who are going to write about you in the history books. We are the ones who get to decide how you will be remembered. So my advice for you is to choose wisely.'

So while Thunberg has gone on the record as saying that her strikes *'achieved nothing'* – because emissions are still rising – we'd beg to disagree. Her passion and determination, and the fact that she cares so much, have made people all over the world sit up and take notice – including those who have the power to bring about change.

Shift 9: From global pandemic to global possibility

The Covid-19 pandemic changed everything, for everyone, everywhere, and triggered a huge, collective shift in the way people see the world, and how they behave within it. As we seek to create better businesses that will thrive within this new landscape, it's the perfect moment to explore what has changed, and work out how to build on what we've learned.

Looking ahead to the post-pandemic world

As everyone's favourite wise old owl Albert Einstein reportedly said, '*In the midst of every crisis lies great opportunity*'. And while no one would ever claim that the events of 2020-21 are worth repeating, we would be foolish if we failed to learn from the experience.

Here are five shifts that we anticipate will make the post-pandemic world we're building better than the pre-pandemic one.

1. The pursuit of a gentler capitalism

According to the United Nations Conference on Trade and Development, 2020 saw a 4.3% contraction in global GDP. The ripple effect of this economic downturn, triggered by Covid-19, has hit the most vulnerable particularly hard, with over 130 million more people struggling with extreme poverty than in previous years.

This growing global gap between rich and poor (which we explored in more detail in Shift 4) is leading people to question the validity of capitalism, with some even suggesting that it's no longer fit for purpose. And while we'd argue that not even a global pandemic could completely overthrow such a deeply embedded system, it's becoming increasingly clear that it might need a health check.

This view existed before Covid-19; in 2019, Business and Society Journalist Oliver Balch noted in the Guardian newspaper: *'For decades, business has been all about maximising profits and keeping owners happy. Now, thousands of companies and organisations are experimenting with broader values – purpose over profit, staff and communities ahead of shareholders – in order to meet the mood of the times.'*

But post-Covid, the calls are getting louder. In 2021, Baroness Minouche Shafik[13] (the director of the London School of Economics), called for a fresh social contract that will bring communities closer together to face our collective challenges. And Mark Carney, former governor of the Bank of England, wrote a book championing a values-based world, in which he argued that we can *'make capitalism better'* by recognising the power societies can have when individuals acknowledge the collective good, instead of focusing on themselves.[14]

So how much more powerful would it be if businesses did the same? They're starting to; some are investing in strategies to help achieve zero-carbon, or carbon-neutral status, while others are considering how to provide genuinely useful services for communities.

Take IKEA, for example, who launched a UK-wide service in 2021 to buy back used IKEA furniture, paying up to 50% of each piece's original value, and reselling them in stores and via Gumtree. This is just one part of their parent company's work to achieve a climate positive value chain by 2030; other global goals include switching to 100% renewable electricity by 2020 and 100% zero-emission home deliveries by 2025.[15]

IKEA will still make a profit; we'll all still love their flatpacks and their eco-lightbulbs. But their impact on the planet will be gentler as a result.

2. The growth of international co-operation

A global crisis requires a global response; and sure enough, Covid-19 proved to be a historic test of international co-operation. It turns out there's nothing quite like a deadly virus to kick-start radically different behaviour.

Faced with the prospect of a terrifying global death rate, a combination of academics and multinational pharmaceutical companies delivered the fastest ever creation of a series of vaccines – without financial margins driving the balance sheet. And leading the charge was Professor Sarah Gilbert, Professor of Vaccinology in the Nuffield Department of Medicine at the University of Oxford.

Building on her pioneering work understanding both the Sars (2002) and Mers (2012) coronaviruses, Professor Gilbert collaborated with Chinese scientists, who shared the genetic code of Covid-19. This led to the creation of the world's first globally approved vaccine, and won her the RSA Albert Medal.

And at a national level, in the UK, two different worlds collided to bring about radical change. The military and medical professions jointly created the Vaccine Taskforce, a hit squad that included Nick Elliott, a former army bomb disposal engineer, and pharma-focused venture capitalist Kate Bingham, who gave her time for free, as well as the very best of our NHS and academic researchers.

This mash-up of diverse and brilliant minds delivered the fastest national rollout of Covid-19 vaccines in the world. And their speedy problem-solving methodology proved so successful that it is being applied to other British Government departments in the hope of replicating their success.

It seems that, when it's a matter of life or death, and the people in charge put people and purpose ahead of profit, global enterprise scrubs up pretty well.

3. The prioritising of health and relationships

As governments across the globe imposed varying degrees of lockdown, it provided an opportunity for us all to take stock and reflect on the way we spend our time and live our lives. And for many, this led to soul-searching about our priorities and personal wellbeing.

For those of us who were required to work from home, and therefore able to skip the 1-3 hour average daily commute, the realisation of how else we could use that time was a massive eye-opener. It may have been temporary – though at the time of writing, a universal return to full-time office work still looks unlikely – but it was a glimpse of what life could be like if we stepped off the capitalist treadmill.

So what did we all do with the extra time? More exercise, for starters; 858,000 people in the UK downloaded the NHS-backed Couch to 5K app between March and the end of June 2020 (a 92% increase on the previous year). More of us were able to accommodate pets into our lifestyles, which has been shown to improve mental and physical health.[16] While baking your own sourdough might not feel like a productivity win, it's a great example of how people slowed down and took a more mindful approach to living.

There were also reports of improved sleep, mental health and productivity, and of people enjoying spending more, unhurried time with their nearest and dearest, even if over Zoom. A surprising outcome was the rediscovery of the joy of talking over tapping; Ofcom's 2020 *Mobile Matters* report noted that the typical mobile phone call had almost doubled in length during lockdown.

Overall, then, the pandemic created space for people to find time for each other, rejecting the *always on* surfing of endless texts, emails and other smartphone notifications, and choosing instead to make time to really, truly, be there for each other. Long may it continue.

4. Recognition for the real heroes

Of course, while some of us were fortunate enough to benefit from this extra time, a huge chunk of the population had the opposite lockdown experience.

People such as our wonderful, and permanently undervalued, NHS staff. Our firefighters, police, emergency responders, teachers, nursery nurses, care assistants and social workers, food chain workers, supermarket workers, postal workers, vets and veterinary nurses, and those in the funeral sector. Our gas, oil, electricity, water and sewage workers, and those working in telecoms and broadband, financial services, and passenger and freight transportation.

These key workers, in their key roles, kept everything going, often under tough conditions and at high risk to their own safety. As we questioned what is important, and reconnected with the values of good health, wellbeing, safety, security and community, we became more appreciative of those who make these things possible.

So while clapping and rainbow posters can never, and should never, be a substitute for fair wages, the pandemic did at least prompt us to recognise these fantastic people for the heroes they really are. To everyone on our far from exhaustive list, we have three things to say. Thank you. We salute you. And we hope that this recognition never fades.

5. A breathing space for the planet

The pandemic caused the steepest slowdown in human activity since the Second World War. With factories closed, cars parked up, planes grounded and many of us confined to our homes, there was a sharp decline in global emissions, which gave our planet the chance to breathe.

No, this didn't put climate change into reverse – but it did take the pressure off the accelerator. In China, the country with the world's biggest carbon footprint, emissions were cut by a quarter. In Venice, the usually rammed waterways became cleaner and clearer than they have been for years, encouraging schools of fish to return.

Indeed, with humans in isolation, and causing less trouble, cautious animals began to show up in places they'd never been seen before: Sika deer in the streets and subway stations of Japan; raccoons on the beaches of Panama; dolphins off the southern coast of Italy.

While it's unlikely that this will lead to a worldwide emission-free lifestyle, the pandemic has at the very least shown what can happen when we slow down our rate of destruction.

OVER TO YOU...

Human beings are creatures of habit and our habits have been significantly changed by the pandemic. We have become keenly aware of the impact of unhealthy practices, and of the transformational effect of swapping them for better ones. And we have learned that we are far from powerless to affect our future.

History has repeatedly shown us that the human race has an unparalleled ability to innovate and engineer change. But what if we brought about this change without waiting for a crisis?

As business leaders, we can instigate radical and purpose-driven initiatives within our organisations at any time. We can work together to re-establish business as a force for good, and create better business, on purpose. We don't need to wait for the next pandemic; our work should begin now. How will you get started?

"Plant trees you'll never see."

Indian Proverb

BBOP in action: Buurtzorg

Dutch healthcare organisation Buurtzorg is an unfeasibly strong example of an autonomous organisation, and a fully-fledged member of Team Teal.

In 2006, Jos de Blok, Gonnie Kronenberg and Ard Leferink founded Buurtzorg out of frustration. They were working for patient home-care companies, built on traditional command-and-control principles which actually got in the way of helping patients.

To give just one example of the nonsensical approach they were up against, time was allocated to patients based on statistics and averages, rather than individual needs, forcing caregivers to pick the most important issue and ignore the rest (e.g. administering medicine vs making a cup of tea vs having time to talk and support).

They knew there must be a better way. So they built Buurtzorg on a purpose, To help people live meaningful, autonomous lives, and three guiding principles: humanity above bureaucracy, simplicity above complexity and practical above hypothetical. They were determined to revolutionise the industry by proving that alternative management, founded in freedom, trust and autonomy, would benefit everyone, especially the patients.

How did they do it? Well, instead of a traditional hierarchy, Buurtzorg has a network of self-managing teams. Every time a team grows to 12 nurses, it splits into two. The two new teams grow until they reach 12 and split again, and again and again. There are no planning, HR or marketing departments, allowing exponential growth without layers of bureaucracy.

And what growth! From a standing start of just four nurses, Buurtzorg now have over 11,000, split into around 900 teams. They also have a 50-person

HQ support team (0.4% of the total workforce) and 20 coaches to help nurses with problems they cannot initially solve themselves.

Everything relevant is shared on the self-developed intranet, helping people in unfamiliar situations to get guidance, enabling others to share information and advice, and allowing CEO Jos de Blok to communicate with everyone at lightning speed.

As a result, Buurtzorg outperform every Dutch competitor, on every imaginable metric. They have the highest client satisfaction of any home-care nursing organisation (by over 30%) and their overheads are 67% lower. Staff turnover is half the rate of their competitors, and staff absenteeism is 33% lower.

And to finish with the most important of them all, Buurtzorg cure patients faster than anyone else in the sector. Proof, beyond question, that autonomy rules.

With thanks to Corporate Rebels for bringing Buurtzorg to our attention.

SECTION 2

SHIFTS IN DOING

BBOP Insight: Beware the inertia of doing

Whilst we're loath to generalise, it's a fair assumption that most purpose-led founders are driven to create a business that acts as a force for good.

And in the early stages, when they're planning what that might look like, they allow themselves to dream. They dream of a company based on their vision, filled with passionate, fulfilled employees, living the art of the possible, unrestricted by limits around the scale of positive impact and value that the business can create.

Then, the work starts. The treadmill starts whirring, everyone focuses on delivery and forgets where they started, and the days start to look the same. The vision starts to fade and the dreams get hazy. There's no time to look around or change lanes, for fear that the wheels could fall off at any minute.

We call this *'The inertia of doing'*, and it's a trap that's remarkably easy to fall into; after a while, it starts to feel normal. The good news is, you can climb out at any time, by making a commitment to do the right things, and doing them differently.

There are thousands of books, blogs and podcasts giving advice and inspiration on how to tackle these issues; a tyranny of choice which can lead to a whole different kind of inertia. But strip it all back, and it's simpler than you might think. We believe that the secret is to focus on seven core aspects of your business, and work towards getting them in balance. Read on to find out how.

THE 7Ps – THE SHIFTS THAT WILL TRANSFORM YOUR BUSINESS

FROM → TO

PURPOSE

MAXIMISING PROFIT → MAXIMISING IMPACT

POSITIONING

PRODUCT POSITIONING → A POSITION OF TRUST

PEOPLE

ASSETS TO BE SWEATED → INDIVIDUALS TO BE CELEBRATED

PRODUCT

'IF YOU BUILD IT, THEY WILL COME' → 'BUILD IT PURPOSEFULLY AND THEY WILL COME'

PROFIT

MAXIMISING PROFIT → MAXIMISING YOUR PROFIT'S POTENTIAL

PLANET

TAKING OUT → PUTTING BACK IN

PLATFORMS

LIMITED IMPACT → LEVERS OF GROWTH

Introducing the 7Ps

In the first part of this book, we focused on the **shifts in thinking** that would help you build a Better Business On Purpose. Having (hopefully) tuned in to a wavelength that will help you create strong foundations, the next step is to focus on the **shifts in doing** that will bring these thoughts to life and ensure that your business is a force for good. But first, you need to understand where to invest your efforts.

If you listen to the advice from business schools and corporate growth books, you might have the impression that the doing you need to focus on is one-dimensional: delivering growth for shareholders. However, if you're building a BBOP, that's not enough. There are actually seven dimensions of doing that you need to consider; they are:

→ **Purpose** – knowing why your business exists beyond just making money, and being sure about the difference you are trying to make in the world.

→ **Positioning** – being clear about what you stand for, and communicating it thoughtfully and effectively.

→ **People** – ensuring your stakeholders are aligned to your purpose, engaged in your mission and treated with respect.

→ **Product** – creating items and services that improve people's lives whilst earning a fair return.

→ **Profit** – investing the money you generate to fuel your purpose and become a force for good.

→ **Planet** – having a net positive impact on the world and the communities who live in it.

→ **Platforms** – using the smartest solutions to scale your positive impact.

We also recognise that in order to become a BBOP, there is a fundamental change to the typical way that each of the 7Ps are traditionally understood. It is this shift that we shall focus on – identifying who is blazing a purpose-led trail, and who is not. We will also, 'P by P', show you how to apply this shift to your business.

The PQualizer: the ultimate balancing act

Just considering the 7Ps isn't enough either; critically, you also need to keep each in balance with one another. If that sounds like a plate-spinning act that might end with smashed crockery, the good news is, we've created a tool to help: the PQualizer.

Meet the PQualizer:

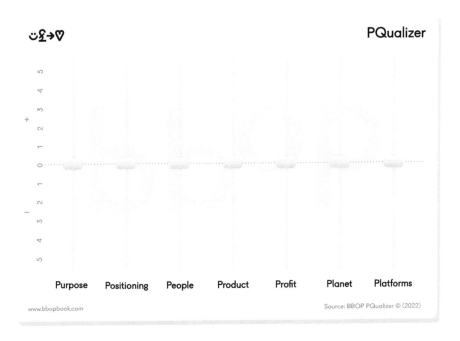

Imagine a graphic equalizer, in which each frequency band of the sound has a slider. When the elements are out of kilter, and one or more dominates at the expense of the others, it's an insult to your ears. Whereas, when all the elements are in balance, you hear a beautiful, complete and well-rounded sound.

The PQualizer works in the same way. It's a framework for ensuring that each of the 7Ps is being actioned in the right proportion, without negatively affecting the others. Like this:

And, just as with a graphic equalizer, the balance is critical. While it's important to have your Ps towards the top of the scale, it's MORE important to have them all at a similar, positive level. Having 3s across the board, for example, is better than having some of the Ps at a 5, a few at a 3 and a couple lurking down at zero.

It's also worth noting upfront (and we'll remind you about it as you go through the chapters) that your purpose should feed into each one.

What the PQualizer is (and isn't)

The PQualizer isn't a scientific piece of equipment. It's a tool that we've created to help you start a conversation around what is and isn't working for your business at a moment in time, based on your knowledge and instincts. Once you've had that conversation, it's a springboard for changing things for the better.

Similarly, the examples we will share with you during this book are not based on definitive, factual scores, or data from the organisations involved. They are relative scores, based on desk research and our external viewpoints, created to illustrate the negative impact of letting the 7Ps get out of kilter, and the transformational result of getting them back in line. Here's one to start you off.

When Volkswagen's balance went from bad to worse

If we were asked to estimate what Volkswagen's PQualizer would have looked like in 2015, before the emissions scandal (where VW exhaust emission ratings were illegally manipulated to be better than they actually were, to sell more cars, which meant they were knowingly putting more carbon into the atmosphere), we'd put it like this:

Volkswagen 2015 (Pre-Emissions Scandal)

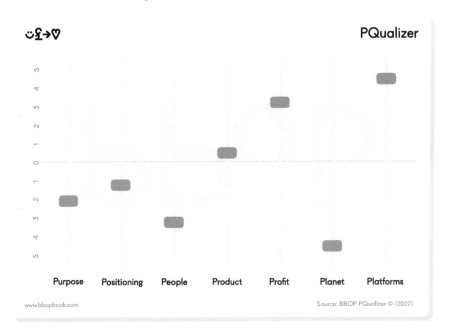

As you can see, there was too much focus on **profit** and **platforms**, at the expense of anything to do with **planet**, **purpose** or **people**.

Now, if Volkswagen had been aware of this, and had taken action to bring all of the 7Ps to a similar level (somewhere around a 2), they would have been in a position to address the emissions issue before it became a scandal.

Instead, it was buried, then leaked, became public knowledge, and had a devastating impact.

Volkswagen were found to have violated the USA's Clean Air Act and were forced to pay for it, including more than $2.7 billion into a fund for environmental remediation, and $2 billion into a fund to be used to promote zero-emissions vehicles.

CEO at the time, Martin Winterkorn, had to pay VW $14m for his lies – after an investigation found the former CEO failed to respond properly to signs that the company may have been using illegal diesel engine technology (source: CNN).

Sales fell off a cliff and the company's reputation was trashed, as the post-scandal PQualizer shows:

Volkswagen 2015 (Post-Emissions Scandal)

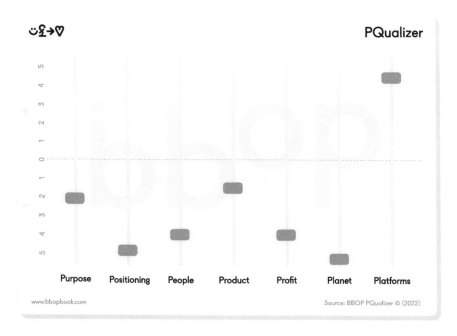

How to use the PQualizer to make your business sing

Clearly, then, if your aim is to build a BBOP, keeping your PQualizer in balance is mission-critical. But first, you need to understand why each one is important, and how they interlink – and that's what this part of the book is all about.

Over the next seven chapters, we'll explore each of the 7Ps in turn, showing you examples of purpose-led businesses who are excelling at keeping theirs in balance, as well as some who clearly have room for improvement. We'll also build the 7Ps Manifesto, chapter by chapter, so you have a simple framework on which to build your Better Business On Purpose.

As we cover each of the 7Ps, you'll be invited to score how your business is performing. Each section contains a scoring plan for the relevant P, to help you build and maintain a PQualizer of your own.

Are you ready? Then let's dive in.

1 PURPOSE

1.1 Purpose: From maximising profit to maximising impact

Know why you exist. Be clear about your business purpose, to create a strong guiding force for every decision. For purpose to have meaning, it must be connected to strategy – it is essential for innovation and reinforced during times of disruption. And there is always disruption.

What we'll explore:

What it looks like when you get purpose right

The impact of getting it wrong

Heads up: Why purpose matters

As the name suggests, purpose is integral to building a BBOP. And, as we noted in our definition right back at the beginning of the book, there are two dimensions to it. The first is the meaningful impact you're seeking to deliver; the second is the deliberate approach you're taking to do so.

When you're driven by purpose, and also building your business on purpose, everything clicks together. This provides you with staying power and helps you make hard decisions, rather than avoiding them. People who share your purpose will gravitate towards you and become a tribe of advocates, creating a wave of opportunity that will drive you onwards. While you may at times get knocked off course, this two-dimensional purpose will help guide you in the right direction.

If you haven't founded your business on purpose, that's OK – it's never too late to start. If you have, but you're not sure whether you're manifesting it properly, that's OK too. Here's how to get it right.

1. What it looks like when you get purpose right

Purpose is a concept that many people find hard to pin down. It's often confused with a company's mission statement or vision, but all three are distinct elements that make up a company's DNA, and it's important to understand why.

In their book *Conscious Capitalism*, John Mackey and Raj Sisodia offer this definition:

→ Purpose refers to the difference you are trying to make in the world

→ Vision is a vivid, imaginative view of what the world will look like once your purpose has been largely realised

→ Mission is the core strategy that must be undertaken to fulfil that purpose

Or, to simplify it further:

→ Purpose is your **why**

→ Vision is your **what**

→ Mission is your **how**

Now, you might think that if you start with the purpose, the rest will follow. But actually, all the elements need to be baked in.

People won't join your tribe of advocates just because they align with **why** you're doing something. They also need to see, understand and believe in your vision (your **what**) and the way you're delivering it (your **how**). In return, just as your customers understand your business, you need to fully understand **who** they are too.

Tesla and the art of purpose creation

A real-life example of how to build in all these elements from the start is Tesla, founded by Elon Musk. In 2006, he wrote a blog post called 'The Secret Tesla Motors Master Plan (just between you and me)', which is a great example of communicating the **why, what, how** and **who** of a business.

As he explained, right up front, *'The overarching purpose of Tesla Motors (and the reason I am funding the company) is to help expedite the move from a mine-and-burn hydrocarbon economy towards a solar electric economy, which I believe to be the primary, but not exclusive, sustainable solution.'*

Musk's master plan clearly set out his purpose, and how the elements were balanced:

Why: To build a carbon-neutral world

What: Electric cars (and, over time, zero-emission electric power generation options)

How: Build a sports car; use the profit to build an affordable car; use *that* profit to build an even more affordable car...

Who: Anyone who strives to be energy positive, starting with climate-conscious drivers (and, over time, bringing in automotive industry laggards)

Clearly, Tesla's purpose is more audacious than most – but that shouldn't put you off. The principles can be carried across to any BBOP, of any shape or size, whose leader is willing to take the time to define their **why, what,**

how and **who.**

How Tesla scores on the PQualizer today

Based on the above, if we were to rate how Tesla scored for purpose on the PQualizer when they started out, we'd put it at a 5. This was, and still is, highly unusual for a new business – and is hard to keep up.

So how has Tesla's purpose endured, and how does it balance with the rest of the 7Ps? Below is how we'd score their PQualizer at the time of writing.

Although **purpose** remains very high, there have been a few missteps. Investing $1.5bn of the company's capital reserves into bitcoin, and then denouncing the *'insane'* amount of energy used to produce bitcoin, wasn't helpful. There are also some serious concerns around the mining of cobalt

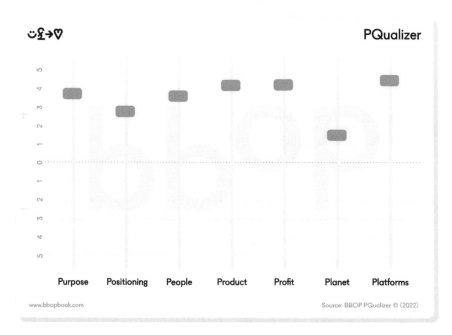

Tesla PQualizer

(one of the main elements in lithium-ion batteries) in the Congo.

However, Tesla are working to address the latter, as part of their drive towards a carbon-neutral world; on balance, we would rate them at a still-high 4.

And this purpose is being well-supported across the other Ps, as our scoring shows:

Product has got better and better; Tesla are adapting and innovating, listening to their customers, and continuing to drive incremental improvement. **Positioning** is strong too, not least because their advocacy is sky-high (although their decision not to invest in marketing or PR leaves them vulnerable).

People is currently strong; but having a CEO with such fierce ambition can drive a work ethic and culture that isn't for everyone. So there may be work to do to sustain this score.

You might expect that **planet** would score exceptionally well. But it's taken a hit, ironically due to the company's success, which led to more new cars being produced, requiring more natural resources. Developments such as a global initiative to recycle older batteries, new business models that allow shared usage of cars, and investment into research and development of new battery technologies, will balance this better.

Profit is ridiculously healthy; at the time of writing, Tesla has a market cap of over $1 trillion (which means they're worth more than the next nine most valuable car makers in total) and an unheard-of gross margin of roughly 30%. All of which supports further investment and innovation.

Platforms are also very strong. Tesla have created a replicable, energy-efficient factory, the 'Gigafactory', to build their cars, and have built supercharger networks across the world to make it easy for people to own them.

Fifteen years in, with several missteps (and some litigation between Musk and his former colleagues) behind them, Tesla are by no means perfect. They still have work to do to get their Ps in balance. But the way their overriding purpose feeds into each of the other Ps means they are better set up for success.

2. The impact of getting it wrong

As the Tesla example shows, the 7Ps all interplay with one another. Profit can't be high without platforms being exceptional. People can't be high without purpose being strong. Positioning will struggle when product is weak. And so on, throughout the 7Ps.

But the single biggest driver of a BBOP is purpose; and if it isn't clear and coherent, every other element suffers. Let's take big oil companies as an example.

When they started out, they drove radical change in the way that Tesla does today; fuelling and enabling human progress by powering the industrial revolution. Today, people all over the world still rely on the oil, petroleum and diesel that the oil companies produce to keep us warm, power our homes and enable worldwide supply chain distribution and travel.

It has become increasingly clear that the price of all this is too high; for people, and for the planet. Because they haven't evolved their purpose to match today's challenges, they are heading for moral and literal bankruptcy, supported by an unhealthy dollop of greenwashing (that is, actively trying to appear more sustainable than they actually are, to appeal to ethically focused customers).

Instead, the oil companies need to redefine their purpose, align their other Ps, and shift the way they behave. This will require bold and audacious leadership and a commitment to accept short-term pain, as profitability is likely to be hit hard.

It's a scary prospect, for sure; but in the long term, focusing on purpose is likely to drive profitability. Don't believe us? The market valuation of Tesla now exceeds that of ExxonMobil, one of the planet's largest fossil fuel mega-corporations – and all in less than two decades of growth.

"Present like you care about something other than profit and power, precisely to gain more of each."

Vivek Ramaswamy

The 'Wokenomics' Argument

In Vivek Ramaswamy's *Woke, Inc.* (Swift, 2021), he presents the case that in some quarters magnanimous gestures of corporate social responsibility can be used as a smokescreen by big brands to cover their otherwise ethically challenging behaviour or profit-driven oversights.

'Wokenomics is a powerful weapon for CEOs, which they can readily deploy as a smokescreen to distract from greed, fraud and malfeasance,' he writes.

He states (among others) that Goldman Sachs' recent, yet behind the curve, announcement that they would refuse to collaborate with businesses who do not have diversity on their boards, was a calculated campaign to shield the public from a multi-billion-pound banking scandal around money laundering and the ruling elite of Malaysia (for which Goldman Sachs were found guilty and fined).

As a business owner, you may be hesitant to join the ethical business movement for fear of *'being tarred with the "woke-washing" brush'.*

Using admirable initiatives to obfuscate your own corporate scandals is clearly unacceptable behaviour, but this is not a reason to avoid exploration of your business's purpose-led agenda.

Our advice here is simple: firstly, behave ethically in the first place; and secondly, ensure that your purpose-led gestures run deeper than a surface-level press release on a current media-led topic of discussion.

Businesses are fast to jump on bandwagons, but the resulting – often empty – statements of intent do little to effect genuine societal change. Name an issue – and most brands are quick to indicate their level of support. But how many actually follow through on these promises with any tangible results? Don't let this be you.

Choose your causes carefully, ideally have them intrinsically linked to your business, your products and/or your team. Do so with genuine intent and integrity. Hold yourself and your business accountable for the changes that you promise to make, their effectiveness and the pace at which you roll them out.

Who else is getting purpose right?

There are a number of great examples of other companies, like Tesla, which stand out because of their 'on purpose' credentials.

An early example of a purpose-led business is **The Body Shop**, founded when Dame Anita Roddick opened her first shop in Brighton back in 1976. Unlike most other high-street retailers, **The Body Shop** had a very clear purpose: to only sell products with ethically sourced, cruelty-free and natural ingredients. While many companies now boast similar eco-credentials, this purpose-led approach was rare at the time; it set The Body Shop apart in a crowded market and drove incredible growth. By 1984, with 138 stores, the business went public; in 2006, it sold to L'Oréal for £652.3 million. As a force for good, The Body Shop packs a powerful punch.

More recently, there's **Peloton**, which at a glance might appear to be selling just another exercise bike. But in reality, the company is a behaviour change platform with clear aims: *'Empowering people to be the best version of themselves'* and *'Using technology and design to connect the world through fitness'.*

In the environmentally challenging world of mobile phones, **Fairphone** are tackling the planned obsolescence that supports a throwaway culture and getting closer to a fairer and more sustainable industry. They offer a five-year warranty, make their products electronic waste neutral, and run a spare parts shop that encourages owners to swap out or upgrade components, rather than replacing the whole device.

As a founder or business leader, it's critical that you're clear on your purpose, and that you're using it to drive your business. It's like a gravitational pull that attracts the right people, partners and opportunities, and repels those aspects that don't fit.

Remember, your purpose is your why – the difference that you're trying to make in the world. Is this clear? Think about your vision when you started the business; what was the impact you were seeking to create? How did you imagine you would go about it? And whose lives were you hoping to change for the better?

If none of this is clear, put finding your guiding purpose, and re-orientating your business around it, at the top of your priority list. Make sure you dedicate time to the process, otherwise it will never happen. Then, once you've got it right, use it as a springboard to bring the rest of your Ps into line.

1.2 Score your Purpose

SCORE YOUR ORGANISATION FOR
POSITIONING USING THE BBOP PQUALIZER

Is the purpose that underpins your business established (intentional) and lived?

Go and ask your most recent employee what difference your business is trying to make in the world – can they tell you?

5	Your purpose is a clear, lived differentiator; it is net positive for the planet and drives positive outcomes for the long term. The company exists to make life better for others.
3	The intent behind your purpose is strong, but not yet fully lived.
1	Your purpose is unclear and not established.
0	Your company has no purpose, or longevity.
-1	Your purpose is confused.
-3	Your purpose is damaging to people and/or the planet.
-5	Your purpose is destructive; it is only driving positive outcomes for a select few, or for no one. Stop what you're doing immediately.

1.3 Purpose in Action

We've explained the pivotal role of purpose for any successful BBOP and explored what it looks like when you get purpose right (and wrong). Now it's time to put these principles into practice. Here are the four key steps that will help you clarify your company's purpose, make it stick, and use it to guide your decision making.

Four steps to shift your approach to purpose

1. Avoid the passion trap
2. Clarify and embed your purpose
3. Align your purpose with the other Ps
4. Move from a reactive to a proactive approach

1. Avoid the passion trap

Before we start exploring what you should do, it's worth a quick diversion into what you shouldn't. It's all too easy to think that passion and purpose are the same thing, not least because *'Follow your passion'* is the basis of hundreds of self-help books and thousands of memes. But they're not, and understanding why is key to avoiding what we're calling the passion trap.

The fact is, while the underlying sentiment is sound, the application is much less so. Following your passion is all about you at the expense of everyone else. Whereas, a well-defined purpose has a clear **who**, a defined group of people which your business will serve, and which keeps you focused on and aligned to the market that you're operating in.

Your market matters, as noted by the multi-talented Andy Rachleff (President and CEO of Wealthfront, lecturer at Stanford Business School, co-founder of Benchmark Capital). Rachleff's Law of Start-up Success says:

'The #1 company-killer is lack of market. When a great team meets a lousy market, market wins. When a lousy team meets a great market, market wins. When a great team meets a great market, something special happens.'

For a BBOP, market matters even more. You can't be purposeful about building a great business without a great market. So you need a **why** that increasingly large numbers of people resonate with, and a **what** that people increasingly want and need.

Does this mean you can't build a business on your passion? Not at all – you just need to approach it from the right perspective. Instead of simply following your passion, find a purpose that you're passionate about, which allows you to put your passion to good use.

Jim Collins sums this up brilliantly in his book *Good to Great*. Using something he calls the Hedgehog Concept, he suggests that what sets great companies apart from failing or mediocre ones is the powerful combination of capabilities, passion and market. The sweet spot where these three elements collide is where you should be rooting your purpose.

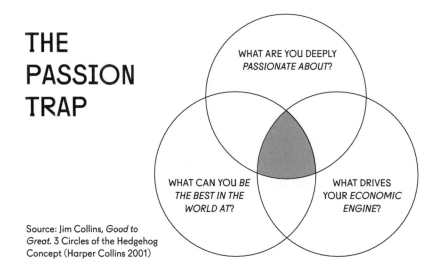

THE PASSION TRAP

WHAT ARE YOU DEEPLY *PASSIONATE ABOUT?*

WHAT CAN YOU *BE THE BEST IN THE WORLD AT?*

WHAT DRIVES YOUR *ECONOMIC ENGINE?*

Source: Jim Collins, *Good to Great*. 3 Circles of the Hedgehog Concept (Harper Collins 2001)

2. Clarify and embed your purpose

If you've read the chapter on purpose in Section 2, you should understand the principles that make a great one. So the next step is to ask yourself whether yours is clearly defined, and embedded in your business. If it's not, you need to step away from the treadmill and take some time out to reflect, because getting it right will be nothing short of transformational.

Here are some questions that you can ask yourself to support this process:

→ When you started, **what** was the dream?

→ **Why** does that change need to happen?

→ **How** are you hoping to achieve it?

→ **Who** is it going to impact? Will they care?

Your answers will help you identify your purpose-building **why, what, how** and **who.** You can also ask your closest confidants how they would answer those questions for you.

Alongside these questions, there are three additional documents you should create. These will help you tell a compelling story of what you want to achieve, in a way that motivates others.

Story Canvas

If you're not familiar with the Lean Business Model Canvas, it's worth checking out. It's a one-page framework that uses boxes to set out the core elements of a new business proposition. So once you've filled it in, you'll have a clear, visual summary of the fundamental building blocks that your business needs.

The Story Canvas follows the same framework approach. But this time, the point is to get clarity on each of the nine building blocks that make up any compelling story.

This is important, because there's real science behind storytelling. Human beings are natural-born storytellers; we've evolved to share information that way. But if you've ever watched a film or read a book and got bored halfway through, it's probably because this science was ignored. A Story Canvas will take you through the process, creating a story of change that your audience will connect with.

You can find out more, and complete a canvas at https://www.bbopbook. com/resources

Vivid Vision

Developed by Cameron Herold, this is a four- or five-page written document which describes your business three years in the future. Herold suggests writing your Vivid Vision somewhere you feel inspired, ideally surrounded by nature, where your imagination can run free.

You should include all the core story-building blocks which you identified in your Story Canvas, and the roles they play in creating that future. It's also worth considering what you hope your PQualizer will look like at that point. Don't worry about how you'll get there, just focus on the three-years-time **why, what, how** and **who.**

Once you've written a draft, pass it on to a writer who can make the words pop. Test it with people that you'd expect to be advocates of your purpose. If their eyes don't light up, ask them why, and use their insights to refine your draft further.

Then be brave and bold and share your Vivid Vision with the world.

Financial model

Having used your Story Canvas and Vivid Vision to bring your purpose to life, you now need to make sure you can deliver it, by creating a robust financial model for each product you offer. There are two ways to approach this, and they're both valid.

The **top-down approach** is particularly helpful from a big-picture perspective, as it shows the full potential of your BBOP within true market conditions. To create a top-down model, you'll need to:

→ Look at the total addressable market (the TAM)

→ Break the TAM down again and again until you can get an idea of how much of that market your business can capture over a period of time

→ This will mean considering the serviceable addressable market (SAM), which is the market that you could capture when considering the competition

→ You will also need to consider the serviceable obtainable market (SOM), which is the part of the market that you can realistically capture.

The diagram on the next page is a real-world example of what this looks like for Airbnb.

However, the risk with the top-down approach is that it's easy to get carried away with your assumptions, which is why some prefer to model their finances using a **bottom-up approach**. This starts with where you are now and explores how and when you can reach your minimum viable audience. (We've covered this in more detail, including how to identify your 1000 true fans, in 'Shifts in Doing: 4 Product - Know your market.')

TOP-DOWN FINANCIAL MODEL

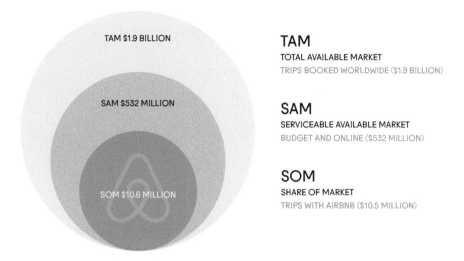

TAM
TOTAL AVAILABLE MARKET
TRIPS BOOKED WORLDWIDE ($1.9 BILLION)

SAM
SERVICEABLE AVAILABLE MARKET
BUDGET AND ONLINE ($532 MILLION)

SOM
SHARE OF MARKET
TRIPS WITH AIRBNB ($10.5 MILLION)

Whichever approach you choose, you should model your revenue, costs, expenses and investments for a three- to five-year period; any more than that and there's too much guesswork involved. Start with annual models, then narrow down to quarterly, and do a monthly version for the next 12 months.

While you will have to make some assumptions, make them as informed as possible. Embrace market research; use search volume data, competitor performance and competitor pricing. Speak to customers and potential customers; their insights are worth a thousand guesses.

It's not a quick process, but by investing time in detailed financial planning, you can be confident that you can embed your purpose in a way that lasts.

Financial model checklist

These are some of the elements to consider when creating your financial model. It's comprehensive, but not exhaustive; there may be other elements specific to your business that need to be taken into account.

→ The market

→ Product variants

→ Product pricing

→ Margin

→ Staff costs

→ Other significant expenses

→ Funding, cash flow, and ROI

→ Which parts of the market you'll serve and when

Once you have the financial model in place, and you're ready to maximise both your profit and your profit's potential, head on over to 'Shifts in Doing: 5 - Profit' where we explore this in detail.

3. Align your purpose with the other Ps

As we explained back in Section 2, the 7Ps don't operate in a vacuum; their power comes from the way they interplay. So once you have all of the above in place, you'll need to make sure that the other 6 Ps are as balanced as possible, and aligned with your central purpose. To make it stick, you'll need to empower your team to call it out if they feel the Ps are slipping out of line.

To remind you: if your purpose is your **why**, the other Ps define your **how**. Of course, the **how** will change over time, as your business evolves. So as you develop your strategy for each of the other Ps, you should update your

Vivid Vision accordingly, to help your community understand where you're heading.

For example, if your people strategy includes a plan to provide jobs for underprivileged communities, revise your Vivid Vision to explain how you see this working, so your advocates can support you in bringing it to life.

4. Move from a reactive to a proactive approach

Once your purpose is clearly defined, you need to take action to bring it to life. This means moving from a reactive to a proactive approach, underpinned by a strategy that commits you to acting as a force for good.

Your Vivid Vision, supported by your Story Canvas and financial model, will support you in this; they will act as a map to help your team understand where you're aiming to get to and encourage everyone to pull in the same direction.

We also recommend building the following principles into your workplan.

Creating and tracking robust KPIs

All successful businesses have a clear benchmarking process in place; for a BBOP, whose goals are far broader than simply financial, it's essential.

The most effective way to do this is to create a set of Key Performance Indicators (KPIs), which ladder back up to your vision. Start with some clear financial measures, then include some non-financial ones which reflect each of the Ps.

It's worth remembering that KPIs aren't something you create and then stick in a drawer; they need to be treated as a live document that develops in line with the business. So create a stupidly simple process for tracking your progress against them, and make sure they're visible to, and understood by, the whole team.

While we're not fans of meetings for meetings' sake, we do recommend building in regular occasions to review your KPIs, alongside your PQualizer scores. Schedule monthly board meetings, attended by both exec and non-exec members, in a setting away from the distractions of the day-to-day running of the business. Use the time to work together to drive action that collectively improves both sets of measures.

Of course, this will be all the more effective if you have the right representatives on board; where possible, select non-execs whose values align with yours and who have experience in building their own BBOPs.

Setting aside time to work on the business

In the early days, we strongly recommend that the founder(s) spend at least half a day each week (and ideally a full day, or more) working on the business itself.

This may sound like a luxury; in fact, it's a critical part of maintaining your BBOP focus. Without it, it's all too easy to slip back into reactive mode and be driven by external forces. So work out which people should be involved in working **on** the business as well as **in** it, and ringfence time and space for them to do so. Not tomorrow; today.

Being deliberate about decision making

The worst type of decision making is indecision. To illustrate the point, here's a quick diversion into ancient history.

In 49 BC, Julius Caesar had to decide whether to re-enter Rome with the 13th Legion, which would trigger a civil war, or to relinquish his command, face exile and end his political career. Standing in his path was the Rubicon, the river he and his troops had to cross to go back into Italy. The river acted as a point of no return, and once Caesar decided to cross it, he was committed to his chosen course of action.

To apply this principle to a business setting, decisiveness is key. So gather the relevant information, then make an active decision, on purpose, and proceed deliberately and rapidly with your execution.

Consciously building on momentum

Of course, making a deliberate decision isn't the end of it; on the contrary, it's just the beginning. Momentum drives momentum; there is always a next move, a next deliberate act that you can take. So make a conscious choice to make each next move, and continue to develop your BBOP.

The next move doesn't have to be a perfect one; no business move ever is. It just has to be a positive one, taken on purpose, and consistent with your purpose.

It doesn't even have to be anything substantial; as James Clear, author of *Atomic Habits,* has noted, frequent tiny gains add up to big ones: *'If you were able to improve by 1% each day for an entire year and those gains compound, you would end up 37 times better at the end of the year.'* Multiply that by your whole team, and the impact could be astonishing.

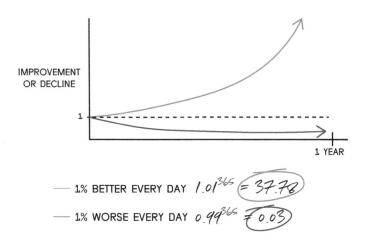

THE POWER OF TINY GAINS

Planning to succeed

As Abraham Lincoln reportedly said, *'Give me six hours to chop down a tree and I will spend the first four sharpening the axe.'* Planning is at the heart of exceptional execution and needs to be part of the culture of any BBOP. Create an environment in which your people focus a considerable amount of time and energy on planning for success, rather than just diving in.

Developing empathy within your team

Back in the 1970s, the Dutch national team transformed the beautiful game with a novel tactical system known as Total Football. As well as being taught to play in their designated positions to an excellent standard, they were trained to play in all the others to a competent one. This created a deeper level of empathy throughout the team; for example, the defenders understood how best to place the ball for the midfielders, because they'd played in that position, and knew how they'd like to receive the ball.

It's a principle that applies really well to a BBOP. If your salespeople understand how to execute a marketing campaign, they'll integrate and collaborate with marketing much more effectively. So encourage and facilitate your people to learn new positions in your business, and reap the rewards.

In short

A BBOP without a clear purpose isn't a BBOP at all. So if you haven't yet pinned down what's driving you, now is the time to start. Begin by defining your purpose, then create a framework for ensuring that it's understood by everyone in your team and embedded within your action plans. Make sure it aligns with the other 6 Ps, and build a culture in which acting proactively, and challenging misalignment, is not only expected but championed.

1.4 Purpose: jump off points

→ How clear is your purpose to you?

→ What are the **what, why** and **who** that underpin your business?

→ Is your purpose as clear to your stakeholders as it is to you?

→ Do your customers understand what your purpose is?

→ Is there any part of your business that doesn't align with your purpose? If so, can you either realign it or stop doing it?

→ What measures do you have in place to allow your stakeholders to challenge actions that might not be aligned?

**NOW RE-SCORE YOURSELF
ON THE PQUALIZER:**

② POSITIONING

2.1 Positioning: From product positioning to a position of trust

Get clear on what your business stands for, and be deliberate about how you communicate it. Strong, purpose-led positioning propels you and your team forward with intent, whilst simultaneously connecting you with your customers.

What we'll explore:

1. What it looks like when you get positioning right

2. The impact of getting it wrong

Heads up: Why purpose-led positioning rules

Good positioning is marketing messaging that is purpose-led, clear and easy to understand; and it's yours for the taking if you follow these three principles:

1. Put your purpose front and centre in your internal and external messaging.

2. Take the time to form and maintain relationships with current and future customers, so they become your brand advocates.

3. Bring the two together with clear, simple and accurate marketing, which connects you with your audience and builds trust.

By shifting your positioning from selling your (high-quality) products to promoting your philosophy, people will be clear on what your business represents and stands for. In a neat twist, that will make more of them want to choose you.

1. What it looks like when you get positioning right

It's been estimated that, in 2021, the average person encountered between 6,000 to 10,000 ads every single day (almost double the figure from 2007). With so much competition for our attention, great positioning is key. Newish kid on the loo-roll block, the Australian company Who Gives a Crap (WGAC), is an excellent example of how to get it right.

In 2012, having discovered that 2.4 million people (approximately 40% of the world's population) don't have access to a toilet, and that almost 300,000 children under five die each year from diarrhoeal diseases caused by poor sanitation, three friends got together to launch a company with a simple agenda: Make. A. Difference.

The result is WGAC, a toilet paper company that doesn't just sell toilet paper (and other paper products). They donate 50% of their profits to help build toilets and improve sanitation in the developing world. Critically, they do so with a healthy dose of toilet humour.

WGAC started as they meant to go on, with an unforgettable crowd-funding launch campaign film, featuring co-founder Simon on a toilet, refusing to budge, until the company had raised enough to go into production. Their marketing has remained bang on ever since, driving forward their sales and enabling them to donate over $10m AUS.

What are WGAC getting right?

WGAC have chosen not to compete on price. They know their audience: people looking to make ethical choices for their household supplies. It's a passionate and ever-expanding global market, and they tap into it brilliantly.

Although they understand that their authentic purpose (bringing sanitation to the masses) is at the core of the product, they never take the moral high-ground or suggest that they or their customers are superior. Instead, they infuse their messaging with on-brand humour and positive messaging, from their strapline (*'Good for your bum, great for the world'*) to their nattily designed packaging, amusing product write-ups and super-engaging emails.

Their blog, *'Talking Crap'*, juxtaposes light-hearted frippery with detailed reporting on how good sanitation can impact communities. The bottom few rolls in each box have a very different style of wrapping, warning their customers to *'Re-order today from whogivesacrap.org or risk getting caught with your pants down'*.

WGAC is a simple **purpose**-driven idea, beautifully **positioned**; and as you can see on the previous page, it scores well on the PQualizer across the other Ps too.

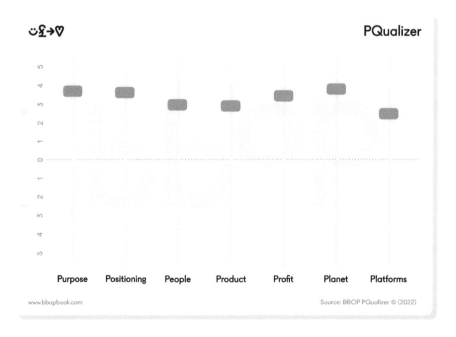

www.bbopbook.com

Source: BBOP PQualizer © (2022)

Their **product** is an essential commodity; one which is unlikely to become obsolete any time soon. And it generates enviable amounts of **profit**, enough for WGAC to remain viable as a business despite giving half of it away. This is supported by their use of the most up-to-date technology **platforms** to sell directly to their growing audience.

And unsurprisingly for a company built around a desire to improve lives all over the **planet**, their consistently high ratings in company culture surveys demonstrate their commitment to **people** within and beyond the organisation.

WGAC's example shows clearly that purpose-led positioning, combined with making sure the other Ps are in line, is a powerful way to do business. They may not be achieving a straight set of 5s, but most people would agree that they're a force for good.

Who else is getting positioning right?

Pedigree, the dog food provider, were losing market share and struggling to create a point of difference between themselves and their many competitors. So, they shifted their positioning to tie the brand's image to something larger; essentially, being *'for dogs'*, which they summed up in their customer manifesto, aptly named *Dogma:*

We're for dogs.

Some people are for whales, some are for the trees... we're for dogs.

The big ones and the little ones. The guardians and the comedians. The purebreds and the mutts.

We're for walks, runs and romps. Digging, scratching, sniffing and fetching.

We're for dog parks, dog doors and dog days.

If there were an international holiday for dogs, on which all dogs were universally recognised for the quality and contribution to our lives, we'd be for that too.

Because we're for dogs.

Dogs rule.

As VP of Marketing, Chris Mondzelewski, noted in 2015, *'We have a fundamental belief that dogs do an enormous amount of good for society... and studies that show this statistically. So if we do good for dogs, obviously through the food we're providing, but also through shelter work, it will resonate with our consumers. If they see us doing that, we become a brand with a mission they want to buy into as well.'*

This philosophy has been playing out through all Pedigree's communications ever since.

2. The impact of getting it wrong

British Airways is a clear example of what happens when positioning gets out of kilter. While some of the company's problems are due to circumstances beyond their control – including competition from cheaper rivals and the slings and arrows of the Covid-19 pandemic, which have hit the entire travel industry – it's fair to say that the decisions they have made have not helped matters.

The once-iconic airline, which championed the quality of their service with their *'We'll Take Good Care Of You'* slogan, is now regarded by many as being in a race to the bottom, trying to beat the budget airlines at their own game.

In a recent annual survey by UK consumer rights advocate *Which?,* ranking the best short-haul carriers, BA has dropped to 15th place (from sixth just five years ago), with some customers damning its business class offering as *'Ryanair but with free food'*. For BA to be compared with a budget airline whose owner promotes cheapness above all else is a dizzying fall.

While it might be obvious in hindsight, championing, promoting and delivering a quality service, rather than trying to copy their low-budget peers, would surely be a better way to maintain their position as providing the best service in the business.

Having got clear on your company's purpose, use every point of contact that you have with the public as an opportunity to champion it. That means infusing what you stand for into all aspects of your positioning, so that your commitment to the greater good comes across as strongly as the quality of your service and products.

If your audience understands the story that your positioning is telling, they're more likely to buy into it, and come on the journey with you. But a word of caution: make authenticity your watchword, as stories that aren't real or, worse still, made up, will have the opposite effect. In our omnichannel world, any inconsistencies in your approach, or gaps between what you say and do, can dramatically undermine how you are perceived.

2.2 Score your Positioning

SCORE YOUR ORGANISATION FOR
POSITIONING USING THE BBOP PQUALIZER

Is your positioning clear? Where are you now? Where are you going?

Consider your business: how would you rate your positioning using the following criteria?

5	Your vision is clear, and is executed with precise positioning that is a market-leading differentiator.
3	Your positioning is clear internally, but needs wider external communication
1	Positioning work is underway internally.
0	No standout positioning in the market.
-1	No comprehensive positioning.
-3	A lack of cohesion between positioning and purpose.
-5	Your positioning is at odds with your purpose, actively detracting from it, and/or is meaningless to others.

2.3 Positioning in Action

We have laid out the importance of being clear about what you stand for as a business, and developing an easy-to-understand, purpose-led positioning that communicates this to all of your stakeholders.

Here we outline the four steps for creating a marketing strategy built on purpose, that will optimise your positioning across all channels, amplify your objectives and build trust between you and your audience(s).

FOUR STEPS TO SHIFT YOUR APPROACH TO POSITIONING

1.	2.	3.	4.
ASSESS THE STATUS QUO	TELL THE MOST POWERFUL STORY	REFRAME YOUR STRATEGY THROUGH A PURPOSE-LED LENS	PUT PRINCIPLES INTO PRACTICE ACROSS YOUR TOUCHPOINTS

1. Assess the status quo

Before you can start looking ahead, you need to take stock of where you are now; you won't be able to develop a strong positioning without understanding how you're currently perceived. You need to:

Clarify what you stand for

In a busy marketplace, businesses that have a well-defined purpose, vision and mission, and communicate them effectively, are the ones that stand out. Explore whether you have defined these clearly enough for your customers, partners and competitors.

Your aim is for them to understand not just what you sell, but why you are selling it, and what greater goals you hope to achieve.

If this information is clear to your stakeholders, they are more likely to believe that you are genuine and become evangelists for your business's purpose and agenda. You can read more about how to define and embed your purpose in the previous chapter.

Assess the perception of your stakeholders

Next, think about how you are currently perceived by your customers, partners and competitors. Are you and your team considered the go-to experts in your field? Providers of the best service? Passionate about what you do? If not, what do you need to change?

If you are seen as offering thought-leading excellence, you will attract and keep more customers, and cement your position as front-runners within your industry.

Compare and contrast your delivery

Finally, look at your different communication channels, and assess the perception you're creating. Is it clear and coherent, within and across each channel? How does your business stack up when seen from all angles?

If you're not expressing yourself clearly to those who work with and buy from you, you're selling yourself short. We'll explore all the different ways that you can share this information, in a way that builds a coherent whole, later in this chapter.

2. Tell the most powerful story

Humans love stories; we're brought up on them as children and spend the rest of our lives seeking them out. The best stories have an engaging narrative, which is why we remember them and share them with others.

But a list of facts isn't a story, and won't engage anyone; no one reads their child the FTSE 500 at bedtime. There's a simple formula for creating a good story that will grab your target customers' or clients' interest.

The best way to think of it is to imagine your customer or client as the hero, and your business, service, or product as the thing which will help them to solve a problem or defeat an adversary; to be victorious, essentially. By doing so, you'll define the value that you provide in a tangible, memorable way.

3. Reframe your strategy through a purpose-led lens

We've already noted the importance of taking a cross-channel approach to reviewing how you're perceived; you need to take a similarly holistic approach to changing the way you operate. As a BBOP, you need to do so with your purpose front and centre. These pointers will help you do just that.

See the four pillars of marketing differently

It's long been established that four pillars underpin all marketing strategies. They are not executions in themselves; they're more of a strategic umbrella, under which all marketing techniques and disciplines sit:

→ **Product** – ensuring your product has unique qualities (see 'Shifts in Doing: 4 - Product' for a more detailed explanation)

→ **Price** – which includes sense-checking your price, your competitors, how people purchase, and the buying mechanism

→ **Place** – understanding from which location(s) you will be selling

→ **Promotion** – making sure people know that they can buy your product

However, viewed through a purpose-led lens, the way to approach them subtly shifts. Rather than promoting the fact that your business makes or sells the *'best'* **product**, the BBOP approach is to focus on providing solutions for your customers' needs and wants, which contribute to the greater good.

Price is then reframed as what your product costs the consumer, and also what it costs to the planet. In terms of **place**, convenience is key: a BBOP's customers should be able to get their product wherever they are in the world. Finally, rather than simply **promoting** their products, BBOPs engage in dialogue with customers and clients on multiple levels, to help them get the information that they need quickly and efficiently.

Don't try to win: be different

BBOPs don't need to destroy the competition or steal a rival's customers; these concepts have no place in a purpose-driven world. Instead, by being clear on your ethical position, the service you provide or the way you put your customers first, you'll make your business stand out as one that your stakeholders can trust.

Similarly, doing what everyone else does rarely gets you noticed; so as a BBOP, you should be willing to take creative risks with your positioning. Brainstorm the resources that you have at your fingertips. Consider the favours you can call in or the celebrity connections you may have. Consider working with experts in insightful engagement-driven marketing to help you define and optimise your messaging.

Understand who your best customers are

Of course, focusing your attention on your target customers is the most productive use of your time and budget. But it's impossible to do so without understanding who they are and what makes them tick.

We recommend creating a minimum of three customer or client personas, basing them on either your favourite existing customers or real people who you believe represent them. You can use this template to map your personas out.

UNDERSTANDING WHO YOUR BEST CUSTOMERS ARE

NAME & ROLE:

INDIVIDUAL CHARACTERTISTICS:
Gender, age, education, family, lifestyle, interests

EXTERNAL PRESSURES:
What others expect of them, targets, who is rating their performance/setting their challenge

INTERNAL DESIRES:
What do they hope to achieve, what do they want out of life, why are they facing a challenge?

WHAT DO THEY NEED FROM ME?
They are in the market for "X", because...

BARRIERS TO BUSINESS:
They are worried about buying from me / working with me because:

A BBOP serves, rather than sells to, its clients and customers. You should also work out what the emotional touchpoints are for your personas, and make sure that your product not only fulfils their needs but also encourages them to trust that you have their interests at heart.

Cherish your super-fans

Super-fans are more than just loyal customers; they are people who are so passionate about your products and/or services that they do your selling for you, becoming unofficial brand ambassadors who recommend you to others.

Statistics show that a word-of-mouth recommendation from a colleague, friend or family member is the most successful way to get someone to change their behaviour. Even a small band of super-passionate fans is a precious commodity, and being clear about your business purpose makes you all the more likely to attract them.

KISS: Keep it simple, stupid

Above all, as you go about firming up your positioning and developing your marketing, make sure your messaging is simple, clear, and super-easy to understand. Remember to communicate the truth behind what you're doing and why you're doing it. Ask yourself regularly: 'If my brand executes this idea, will anyone really care?'

4. Put principles into practice across your touchpoints

It's important to remember that the marketing landscape has shifted dramatically in recent years. Traditionally, it was just a question of getting your marketing materials under the noses of customers or clients, to let them know what you were selling. But in today's digital world, there are countless ways that potential and current customers can interact with your brand.

They can explore your website and social media presence, read online reviews, assess your business ethics and culture, engage with your online communities, see testimonials from your advocates, view film advertising campaigns... and all these different points of contact work together to paint a picture of who you are. They all need to be in line with your positioning, and the purpose that drives it.

As a BBOP, you therefore need to get to grips with this new marketing landscape, understand and identify all the different ways you can be found, and make sure your purpose-led positioning tracks across them. Here are the main touchpoints that you should review with your purpose in mind, to develop a genuine, coherent, cross-channel positioning.

Your manifesto

It's well worth sharing your purpose with your team, partners and customers. Help them understand why your business exists, and how this philosophy runs through every action you take.

Branding

Does your business branding reflect who you are, and where you're trying to get to? Is it true to your purpose? Striking, arresting branding, which is in line with your values and aspirations, will make you more attractive to the people you want to reach.

Website

Your website is essentially your entire business story in one place, so it must offer a window onto your purpose, as well as your offer. It should also, of course, be consistent with your branding, and easy to navigate and buy from.

Social media

Posts that are visually on-brand, in your tone of voice, and underpinned by your purpose, can be a powerful tool for spreading the word about your business and its goals. Make sure your approach is tailored to each specific platform and its distinct audience.

Customer Relationship Management (CRM)

Email marketing is the most cost-effective way to reach customers. As a BBOP, that means creating a dialogue rather than just selling stuff; so find ways to reference your purpose, such as sharing initiatives you are leading or events you have produced.

Film

Films are a brilliant way to assert and establish your positioning to different audience groups across the full range of digital platforms. Make sure they reflect your overarching purpose in a way that's relevant to each audience, rather than just promoting your products and services.

Online communities

Encourage authentic communities of like-minded individuals who share your purpose to gather together, either physically or online, under your banner. These communities take time to become established, but it's usually time well spent.

You may find that your communities can be self-managing, with super-passionate members taking on the responsibility for running the show. More typically, they will need curation (giving members good reasons to show up) and moderation (monitoring conversations and posts to ensure members abide by community rules).

Paid advertising

From more traditional formats such as print media or television to more data-driven, pay-per-click advertising via social media or Google ads, paid advertising should always be part of your communication strategy. Again:

your messaging can set out and celebrate your purpose-driven goals as well as promote your new services or products. Just make sure you refine your approach to match the channel. For example:

→ **Pay-per-click** (PPC) marketing needs to operate at scale and should be continuously tested to maximise effectiveness. So commit to a minimum monthly spend, and run several variations on each advert, to see which one drives the best results.

→ **Creative advertising** is no longer a luxury only affordable by big brands, thanks to the growth of the boutique ad agency. Generally more agile than their global conglomerate counterparts, they tend to be run by ex-global ad agency employees, who are seeking to work with new, purpose-led businesses that are willing to take creative risks.

  - These organisations' creatives tend to be across every aspect of technology; they will be able to fuse more traditional marketing media, art and your purpose data-driven initiatives with the latest developments in artificial intelligence, augmented reality, virtual reality, smart speakers, wearable technology, drones... there are almost no limits to what is possible.

  - As Raja Rajamannar wrote in *Quantum Marketing,* his insightful 2022 book, *"Marketing is a force multiplier"*, the availability of these new technologies, underpinned by great thinking, means there has never been a more exciting time to amplify your message.

  - By partnering with the right agency, you'll be well placed to create an advertising strategy that aligns with your business purpose and drives positive behaviour change, whilst championing your business's agenda, philosophy and products.

→ **Paid media** involves working with the new breed of media companies to get your intelligently targeted adverts in front of the right people. It's worth your consideration, as even the most engaging campaign in the world is all but useless if no one sees it.

- As a subset of paid media, working with YouTube and other social media influencers who share your brand ethics can also help you get your message to your target audience, and lead to spikes in sales.

→ **Earned media**

- Of course, you don't always have to pay for external endorsement. So when your brand and its purpose inspire authentic third-party support, you should celebrate and amplify this. Any independent YouTube review that rates your product or activity highly should be re-shared on your social media channels; don't underestimate the impact of contacting the reviewer personally to thank them.

Thought leadership

Get your team out there to share your purpose in person. Giving keynote lectures, being invited to sit on expert panels, and writing blog posts and magazine articles all allow you to share your knowledge and experience in a way that helps others. The impact that this will have on how you are perceived will seriously help your business, too.

Events

From large-scale, high-price conferences to business breakfasts and weekend retreats, events are another way to share your purpose-led positioning first-hand. Whether you're the host or attending as a guest, just remember to focus on what you're about as well as whatever you're promoting.

In short

Your business's purpose shouldn't be a document that is shoved in a drawer and only looked at from time to time; it should be infused through everything you do and say. That means developing a positioning that clarifies what you stand for and what you're hoping to achieve. It also means ensuring that you're expressing your purpose coherently across all your channels and touchpoints, so that your stakeholders believe that what you're saying is genuine.

Your positioning isn't only about selling products – it's about promoting trust in your brand. If you get the trust right, the products will sell themselves.

2.4 Positioning: jump off points

Questions to spur you into action

→ Are you clear on your company's purpose, mission and vision? Are all your stakeholders?

→ What can you be the best in the world at?

→ Do you have a public-facing manifesto?

→ Have you recently conducted a marketing review?

→ Are all of your communications, across all channels, aligned, inter-related, on-brand and purpose-led?

NOW RE-SCORE YOURSELF
ON THE PQUALIZER:

3 PEOPLE

3.1 People: From assets to be sweated to individuals to be celebrated

Happy, engaged people do better work than miserable ones, and people want to associate with purpose-driven companies, which they believe in and can contribute to. That goes for your team, your customers and those you partner with too. Be deliberate in enabling your people to enjoy their journey with you.

What we'll explore:

1.   What it looks like when you get people right
2.   The impact of getting it wrong

Heads up: Why being purposeful about people matters

What makes people want to work with you? What drives people to join your team, partner up with you or buy from you?

Talented people have choices about where they work, and customers have choices about who they buy from. So making sure both understand your purpose, and that they will benefit from the way it's built into your culture, is a core part of sealing the deal.

It's no secret that having brilliant people on your team gives you a competitive edge. It allows you to provide your clients with exceptional products or services, and your business to grow and evolve at a faster rate. And it helps other brilliant people – potential employees, clients, partners, customers, patients – recognise your success and seek to be part of it.

The fact is, what happens inside the business naturally shapes the experience of partners and customers alike. So you need to take care of your company culture, as it speaks volumes to the internal team, across the industry and right out into the wider world.

1. What it looks like when you get people right

Dutch healthcare organisation Buurtzorg, who we came across in 'Shifts in Thinking: Shift 9', is an unfeasibly strong example of an autonomous organisation.

In 2006, Jos de Blok, Gonnie Kronenberg and Ard Leferink founded Buurtzorg (Dutch for *'neighbourhood care'*) out of frustration. They were working for patient home-care companies, built on traditional command-and-control principles which actually got in the way of helping patients.

To give just one example of the nonsensical approach they were up against, time was allocated to patients based on statistics and averages, rather than individual needs, forcing caregivers to pick the most important issue and ignore the rest (e.g. administering medicine vs making a cup of tea vs having time to talk and provide support).

They knew there must be a better way. So they built Buurtzorg with a **purpose;** *To help people live meaningful, autonomous lives,* with a **product** designed and defined by three guiding principles: *humanity above bureaucracy, simplicity above complexity* and *practical above hypothetical.* The duo were determined to revolutionise the industry by proving that alternative management, founded on freedom, trust and autonomy, would benefit everyone, especially the patients*.*

How did they do it? By being people-first, in terms of both patients and team.

Instead of a traditional hierarchy, Buurtzorg have a network of self-managing teams. Every time a team grows to 12 nurses, it splits into two. The two new teams continue to grow until they reach 12 and split again, and again and again. There are no planning, HR or marketing departments, which allows exponential growth without layers of bureaucracy.

And what growth; from a standing start of just four nurses, Buurtzorg now have over 15,000 of them, split into around 1,425 teams. They also have a 50-person HQ support team (0.3% of the total workforce) and 20 coaches to help nurses with problems they cannot initially solve themselves. All of which feeds into a high and brilliantly balanced score on the PQualizer.

In terms of **planet**, Buurtzorg's resource overhead is far lower than other national healthcare providers, leading to a comparatively lower carbon footprint. With a growing ageing population across the globe driving a growing need for care, this will become more important with every year that passes.

The business is underpinned by a strong communication **platform**. Everything relevant is shared on the self-developed intranet, helping people in unfamiliar situations to get guidance, enabling others to share information and advice, and allowing CEO Jos de Blok to communicate with everyone at lightning speed.

There is room for improvement in terms of **positioning**, in particular the sharing of their story. You may well have heard of Buurtzorg but many others have not; it's tantalising to think of the positive impact on global health if more nation states were aware of the model.

Funding can be a challenge as the Dutch model is tailored to payments through health insurance companies – not a state healthcare system like the UK NHS. However, as Buurtzorg is a social enterprise, any surplus **profits** are reinvested. And their true *'currency'* is patient health outcomes, in which they outperform every Dutch competitor, on every imaginable metric.

Buurtzorg have the highest client satisfaction scores of any home-care nursing organisation (by over 30%) and their overheads are 67% lower. Staff turnover is half the rate of their competitors, and staff absenteeism is 33% lower – the fact that employees select their own leaders, and staff set their own salaries, could be significant contributing factors here.

Critically, Buurtzorg cure patients faster than anyone else in the sector. As the *American Journal of Nursing* reports, Buurtzorg patients improved twice as fast in half the time with one third fewer care visits. Proof, beyond question, that autonomy rules, and that a people-first approach really pays off.

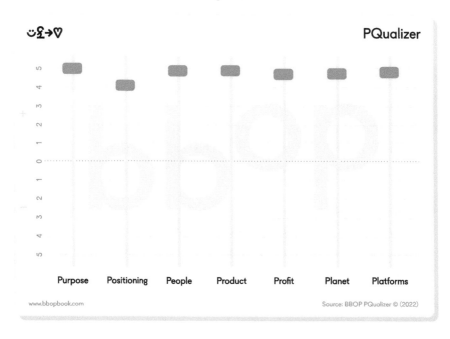

Buurtzorg PQualizer

The great news is that the Buurtzorg approach is being seized on by policymakers as a means of supporting those with care needs to live more independent lives – with potential cost savings of up to 40%. The model is being trialled in the UK, Sweden, Germany and Austria, with the US, Japan, China, Taiwan and South Korea to follow.

On balance, Buurtzorg is well on the way towards BBOP legend status, with an even and high-scoring PQualizer, driven by people-focused innovation and underpinned by a clear purpose.

There are plenty of brands that take their people seriously, and pride themselves on how they treat all those that they come into contact with.

Who else is getting it right?

When the Covid pandemic upturned the travel industry overnight, **Airbnb** co-founder Brian Chesky wrote an open letter to employees explaining the need for 1,900 lay-offs. Ending with the message *'I am truly sorry. Please know this is not your fault'*, the letter typifies how to lead in a crisis.

Brian and his leadership colleagues couldn't control the impact of their (enforced) decision, but they could choose to do it in the gentlest way possible, communicating it honestly and carefully, and offering support to all those whose roles were at risk. They said they were sorry, and their actions helped people believe them.

Similarly, showing how the people outside a business are as important as those within it, online retailer **Zappos** have spent two decades offering legendary levels of customer service. Their core values, which guide how they interact with employees, customers, community, vendors and business partners, are a note-perfect example of treating people right.

2. The impact of getting it wrong

In stark contrast to the people-based wonders of Buurtzorg, there are too many high-profile businesses in which the balance is completely off track. And these two examples show clearly how getting just one of the Ps wrong can impact every other part of the business. How would you score them?

BrewDog

The self-defined punks of the brewing industry, whose carbon-busting, planet-first approach was supposed to be setting new standards for purpose-driven businesses, were outed as the opposite by former employees *'Punks with Purpose'* in 2021.

The open letter about the company's *'culture of fear'* outlined a litany of allegations against BrewDog, describing it as *'A lightning rod for some of the worst attitudes present on both the internet and in real life'* and noting that, for staff, *'Being treated like a human being was sadly not always a given.'*

CEO James Watt responded by issuing a plethora of public apologies and hiring a culture consultant. But the damage was real; the way they were shown to be treating their people had a highly negative effect on their reputation, and put their IPO at risk.

At the time of writing, Watt is taking further action to demonstrate his new commitment to radical transparency. This includes a 'Transparency Dashboard' which sits in plain sight on the BrewDog website. Its headline measures include employee satisfaction scores (currently 3.44/5) and the number of mental health first aiders employed (86), along with others relating to people, planet and performance. It remains to be seen whether this is enough to turn BrewDog's reputation around.

United Airlines

In 2017, United made unwanted headlines when videos emerged of Dr David Dao Duy Anh being forcibly removed from an overbooked flight.

The doctor's suffering – which, according to ABC News, included concussion, a broken nose and two missing teeth – was witnessed by millions of people as the footage was shared on social media. United took a financial hit, losing nearly $1billion in market capitalisation due to their blatant mishandling of a people-related issue.

How would you score these companies on the PQualizer?

People create businesses, not the other way around. So it seems obvious that company cultures and decisions should be rooted in how people are affected, and driven by a desire to see them thrive. That includes those who connect with you as clients, customers or other contacts, as well as your internal team.

It's worth remembering that keeping people on a par with all the other Ps is an ongoing journey, not a one-off statement or a change-management project. How your people-focus lives and breathes will define how you succeed; in today's interconnected world, your customers will be able to see when your business is out of balance – maybe faster than you.

3.2 Score your People

SCORE YOUR ORGANISATION FOR
POSITIONING USING THE BBOP PQUALIZER

Do you have the right people on your team? And are they aligned with your mission?

How would you score your appraoch?

5	Everyone who touches your business, internally or externally, is aligned with your purpose, and becomes an advocate.
3	You have an engaged team, with most of the right people in the right seats, loyal customers and strong enduring partnerships, with some gaps to be addressed.
1	A lack of engagement across and outside the organisation.
0	No engagement, no clear team strategy, low or no customer loyalty, and no clear partnership approach, leading to chaos.
-1	An unengaged, unaligned team who are pulling in different directions, and only transactional customer and partner relationships.
-3	Engagement issues including silo thinking and empire-building, and partners treated like suppliers.
-5	A toxic culture which undermines your mission, creating detractors both inside and out of your organisation.

3.3 People in Action

The impact of putting people ahead of the bottom line, and engaging meaningfully with your team, customers and suppliers will always be net positive. The five key stages of the people cycle that can be transformed by taking a purposeful approach, are laid out in this next section along with our guide on how to apply them to your business.

If engagement is not compelling enough in its own right, consider this: 1/4 of US workers quit their jobs in 2021, despite wage increases and post-lockdown WFH options. The need to prioritise your people has never been greater.

1. Recruit with purpose

According to Randy Street and Geoff Smart, in their book *Who: The A Method for Hiring*, the average recruitment mistake costs a horrifying 15 times an employee's base salary in hard costs and productivity. So hiring the wrong £40k employee could cost you £600k; a huge amount of money, which could be better spent on almost anything else.

Getting it right starts with you, and it's easier than you might think. Use these principles as your guide:

Nobody sells you better than you. If you believe that your purpose might just light up the world, share it with as many people as possible in the most compelling way. Talk it, write it, podcast it; just do it.

Encourage your team to do the same. When someone other than you says how amazing your business, product or service is, potential candidates listen. And when it's your team doing the talking, it dials the authenticity up to 10.

Employ 'always on' recruitment. If you panic recruit, the chances are you'll end up with the (expensively) wrong person. Instead, treat recruitment as an ongoing conversation. Ask everyone in the company to pick the top 10 people they would like to work with, then connect and engage with these people to explore what opportunities could arise.

Make it easy for people to find you. Hang out where your audience hangs out, and engage in meaningful conversations, rather than yelling into the echo chamber of untargeted channels.

Develop a progressive recruitment strategy that supports diversity. Diversity brings strength and supports high impact thinking. And progressive recruitment opens up opportunities to key groups and

FIVE STEPS TO SHIFT YOUR APPROACH TO PEOPLE

1.
RECRUIT WITH PURPOSE

2.
ENGAGE YOUR TEAM AND ALIGN THEM WITH YOUR VALUES

3.
TURN YOUR LEAVERS INTO POWERFUL ALUMNI

4.
KEEP YOUR CUSTOMERS IN THE ROOM

5.
TREAT SUPPLIERS AS PARTNERS

supports workplace equality. So widen your pool of candidates by tackling any unequal or outdated practices which might put people off. This includes:

→ Being clear about what you stand for. A clear anti-racist stance is a far stronger way to drive positive change than simply 'not being racist'.

→ Actively encouraging applicants from underrepresented groups, and being inclusive of protected characteristics. In UK law, this includes age, disability, gender, gender assignment, marriage and civil partnership, race, sexuality, pregnancy and maternity, and religious belief or lack thereof.

→ Considering whether to specify required qualifications. If you don't specifically need a graduate, don't ask for one; you may attract a talented school leaver who wouldn't otherwise apply.

→ Giving people a chance to show their potential. For example, would a demonstration of work be a better indication of ability than a CV?

→ Paying people for their time in going through a recruitment process. This shows candidates that you value their time and allows those on low incomes to take part.

And whatever else you do, show salaries in your recruitment ads. This saves time, effort and money for all concerned.

Use a scorecard

A scorecard may sound a bit corporate, but trust us, it's a gamechanger. It forces you to think clearly about what you're looking for, and how you're going to evaluate this, before any candidates show up for their interview. And it aligns your panel on what 'good' looks like, which drives clean, swift decision making.

We've included a scorecard template below; feel free to adapt it to suit your business.

RECRUITMENT SCORECARD

		Candidate 1	Candidate 2	Candidate 3	Candidate 4
ROLE	Company Purpose: Alignment?				
	Company Values: Alignment?				
	Role Purpose:				
ESSENTIALS	Experience				
	Demonstration of work				
	Role model / Leadership				
	People Focus / Skills focus				
	Industry acumen				
BONUS	Languages / tbc.				

SCORING

3	2	1	0
exceeds expectations for the role	good level of experience	would need support	no evidence/ clarity

As you do so, bear these three things in mind:

→ Ensure you assess for the ability to *do the work* – not just to do a great interview. These are two very different things, and getting it wrong matters.

→ Incorporate questions about purpose and values, as well as skills. The skills you bring in need to be pointing in the right direction, so it's best to have total clarity here from the start.

→ Never forget that an interview works both ways. As a BBOP, your aim is for everyone you come into contact with to come away with a positive, ideally advocate view. So make candidates feel part of the team, create strong feedback loops and short timeframes (talented people get snapped up quickly) and never, ever, ghost anyone.

2. Engage your team and align them with your values

As well as making sure you bring people in who share your purpose, you also need to check whether your existing team are similarly aligned. A simple way to do this is to find out whether your team would champion your company's purpose to others.

We suggest adapting the classic Net Promoter Score question, to ask and score as follows:

'On a scale of 0-10, with 0 being low and 10 being high, how likely would you be to champion our company's purpose to others?'

Score 0-6:   A detractor of your business, likely to have a negative view

Score 7-8:   Passive or neutral, neither actively negative nor promoting your purpose

Score 9-10:   A promoter of your company's purpose

The answers may surprise you; so before you start, ask yourself the following questions:

→ How would you score, personally?

→ How do you think the leadership team would score?

→ What about the rest of the team?

→ Would the leadership team score differently from the rest of the business?

→ What do you think the difference might be?

In 99% of organisations, there is a significant gap between the engagement of the senior team and other groups of employees. So it's worth checking your expectations against the reality – and taking action to address any gaps.

Getting the balance right

Too many companies behave as if engagement is all about fruit bowls and yoga classes. Whereas in reality, people are looking for bold, empathetic, experienced leadership which inspires them to be the best they can be each day.

Now, it's fair to say that creating and maintaining this environment requires a fine balance. Talented people have choices, so if you treat your employees as assets to be sweated, you will create a revolving door of leavers and joiners. But on the flip side, if you make them feel too comfortable, you may stifle their careers and business progress.

So as a BBOP, you should aim to tread the line by creating an environment with a level of pressure that is fit for purpose and allows your people to thrive on the challenge. Personal bests are always beaten under pressure; a healthy amount, within a supportive culture, with a highly engaged team, can deliver outstanding results.

3. Turn your leavers into powerful alumni

Happy, positive leavers are the best brand advocates you can get. They know the inner workings of your business; they are likely to be aligned with your purpose and to have made a positive impact. And if you manage their departure well, they are equally likely to sing your praises on the next step of their journey.

Consultancy firms, while not typically BBOPs, have a strong record in this area, treating their leavers in a similar way to universities and their graduates. They assist with the transition, help set them up for future success and stay in touch through an alumni programme.

For these firms, the main incentive is that their former employees may become future clients. But for a BBOP, it's more about creating a network of advocates who will share your story, enabling your purpose to live beyond the walls of your company.

Here's an 8-point plan for how to lose your talent in the most positive way:

1. Succession plan, constantly, so you don't have to panic when someone decides to move on.

2. Think strategically about what you do next. Do you need a direct replacement, or is it time to rethink the role?

3. If you opt for a direct replacement, involve the leaver in their recruitment. After all, no one knows the role better than they do.

4. Share the news, and the plans, with everyone – including your clients. Finding out after the event won't help people feel engaged.

5. Celebrate when someone leaves. It demystifies the change and turns it into a communal experience. People tend to tell the story of how they are treated on the way out, so give them something positive to talk about.

6. Hold exit interviews. Make them engaging, be clear that you're seeking an honest opinion – and make sure you act on what you hear.

7. If you have to make someone redundant, support them as much as you can financially, emotionally and through contacts for new roles. There are some great examples of this, including Airbnb, who encourage people to add their profiles to their alumni talent directory, which helps them find new roles, even if they have been laid off.

8. Keep the door wide open and the conversation flowing. This will create a collective of ex-employees who become valuable customers, partners, returning employees, mentors to your current team and brand ambassadors to the world.

A strong alumni is a competitive advantage, if you create it on purpose. People will leave, the world will keep turning, and life will go on, so you might as well make it as positive as possible. The good ones never really leave you anyway.

4. Keep your customers in the room

Ask yourself this: do you think of your customers as individual human beings or a homogenous group? And are they 'in the room' when you're making key decisions that directly impact their experience of the business?

As we've noted elsewhere, when it comes to customers, BBOPs should think serve, not sell. Without your customers you don't have a business, so creating value for them should be front of mind.

If you've read the previous chapter, you'll know about creating personas to capture the essence of your best customers. The next step is to share this with the rest of your organisation, so that these personas become almost part of the business.

Once your team is clear on your personas, ask them these questions:

→ Do you bring these personas into the business, especially the boardroom?

→ Do you think about what they would say if they had a voice in the room?

→ Do you prioritise explaining what you're doing to help them and how you're continuing to innovate?

This shift to being customer-driven, rather than transaction-focused, will help your team stay focused on your customers' needs. And this in turn will help you shape your products and services, in a way that benefits everyone.

A brilliant example of this is Pedigree, who we first mentioned in 'Shifts in Doing: 2 - Positioning'. Recognising that people's relationships with their pets are often more emotional than practical, they shifted their focus from *'putting wet food in tins and dry food in bags to make a profit'*, to being *'for dogs'*. And they brought this to life with a customer manifesto, aptly named *Dogma*.

The impact was huge, spanning twelve countries and five continents. Dog-friendly offices sprung to life; new business cards featuring employees' dogs were printed; a canine health plan was created... It was transformational for the company and the team, as well as their customers and canine friends.

Let's give the last word on being customer-driven (aka market-driven) to Seth Godin, author of 18 best-sellers and a member of the Marketing Hall of Fame:

'When you're marketing-driven, you're focused on the latest Facebook data hack, the design of your new logo, and your Canadian pricing model. On the other hand, when you're market-driven, you think a lot about the hopes and dreams of your customers and their friends... Being market-driven lasts.'

5. Treat suppliers as partners

According to John Mackey, Co-CEO of Whole Foods Market and author of *Conscious Capitalism*, as much as 80% of the value the average company provides to its customers is created by suppliers. That's a huge proportion – and one that should be recognised. Suppliers are people too.

Like talented people, talented suppliers have choices in who they work with. So BBOPs should make an effort to seek out suppliers who share their values, and engage with them, just as they do with their staff; ideally, the relationship should be more like a partnership. This includes:

Negotiating purposefully and realistically. Make sure that both parties benefit from the relationship.

Communicating as you would with your internal team. Engage, share your challenges, listen to and act on feedback.

Paying fairly. Look for healthy competition, instead of driving suppliers' pricing so hard that they need to cut corners, reduce quality or end up going out of business. That's a lose-lose for all concerned.

Paying on time, with reasonable terms. Too many companies demand extended payment terms or continually pay late. It's short-sighted, as it puts a strain on cash flow across the entire ecosystem. Do you pay your staff on time? Then extend that courtesy to your suppliers.

A positive example of supplier partnership in action is UK supermarket Sainsbury's, who moved to immediate payment terms for suppliers at the start of the Covid-19 pandemic. They also offered additional support to suppliers who were in financial distress as a result of the ongoing uncertainty. And their shelves stayed stocked as a result.

This approach was the opposite of that taken by many other companies, and clearly illustrates how developing good relationships with your suppliers will build your reputation, which in turn will encourage others to work with you. Much like your internal team, a strong partnership network is a competitive advantage.

In short

When it comes to people, a BBOP sets out to create value for all stakeholders, not just shareholders (whose main interest is the bottom line). Taking this approach will help you attract talent and build collaborative relationships with stakeholders, delivering impact and influence in multiple ways:

→ Your team will become assets that appreciate over time, becoming more engaged and valuable the more you invest in them.

→ When they leave (as they probably will, and should), they are more likely to become advocates and share your story with their growing networks.

→ Your customers will become people that you help, not sell to, which will transform the way you make decisions about your business. And keeping them 'in the room' will help you stay customer-driven, rather than transaction-focused.

→ Your suppliers will become partners, with whom you have mutually beneficial relationships, building your reputation as a partner of choice, and creating ongoing value for your customers.

3.4 People: jump off points

Questions to spur you into action

→ Are your values clear, and embedded into every stage of your recruitment?

→ Are your team aligned and engaged with your purpose? Have you asked?

→ How high is your staff turnover and why do people move on? What can you learn from this?

→ Does the map of your engagement, performance and potential of employees set you up for success?

→ Do you have an alumni programme? How could you celebrate your leavers, their legacy and their continued love of your business and purpose?

→ Do you know who your customers really are? And are they in the room when decisions that directly affect them are being made?

→ Are your suppliers treated like partners, and working with you to create a competitive advantage? Are they proud to have you on their creds?

NOW RE-SCORE YOURSELF ON THE PQUALIZER:

4 PRODUCT

4.1 Product: From 'If you build it they will come' to 'Build it purposefully and they will come'

Make sure your products and services improve lives in ways that earn a fair return for their innovation and impact. And make them stand out from the crowd. That way, they'll compel people to engage, buy, share and recommend them.

What we'll explore:

1. What it looks like when you get product right
2. The impact of getting it wrong

Heads up: Why being purposeful about product is important

Products can fall into all kinds of categories. Your company may offer multiple products, or just one. They may be simple to develop and sell, or highly complicated. They may be tangible items, or services. If you're in the business of reselling, they may even be created by someone else.

But whether you're offering a service or a physical item, created by your company or elsewhere, you need to think of that as your product, and make sure that your purpose runs through it, at every stage of its development.

Although the nature of a BBOP is to change things for the better, change can sometimes feel uncomfortable. So developing purpose-led products means making the change as comfortable as possible for your customers, as well as being enjoyable and memorable so that they're likely to tell others.

1. What it looks like when you get product right

Few brands are as celebrated for their product genius as Apple. At the time of writing, it is one of the biggest and most widely recognised companies in the world, with a market capitalisation of over $2 trillion (that's a lot of zeros).

But it hasn't always been this way. Let's rewind to 1997, and see how we'd have scored their PQualizer back then:

Apple PQualizer - 1997

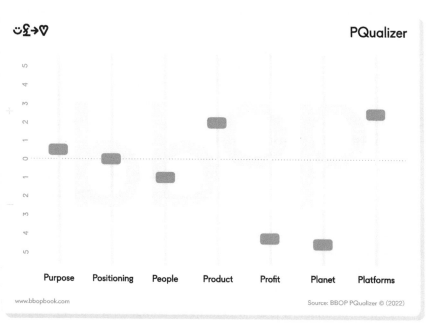

It's immediately obvious that the Ps aren't in balance, and that several are damagingly low. At the time, Apple was in very bad shape; CEO Gil Amelio had recently been ousted and the company was on the verge of bankruptcy. Their $150 million bail-out deal with competitor Microsoft left their positioning in tatters.

Additionally, despite the hippy origins and eco-credentials of founder Steve Jobs and Wozniak, Apple had a huge reliance on coal power and electricity, and was using toxic chemicals and components to build their products. This led to the company scoring just 2.7 out of 10 in Greenpeace's Guide to Greener Electronics report; five years later, they were bottom of the list.

How did Apple turn it around? Three key factors came into play:

1. **The return of Steve Jobs** – and with him, purpose-driven leadership. The impact of this on the company cannot be underestimated; without Jobs' on-purpose reset, Apple would probably have gone out of business.

2. **The ongoing strength of their products**. The Apple II launched in 1977, off the back of strong market reception for the Apple I, which was in retrospect the MVP. In the next three years, annual revenues grew from $7.8 million to $47.8 million to $117 million – an astonishing 1,500% growth.

3. **Their solid platform principles** in which their growth was rooted. Apple had worked out early how to stand out, and how to leverage what they were doing to reach the widest audience.

Although by 1997 the company was on life support, it was succeeding at product, platforms and the Jobs-driven purpose. These three elements provided a springboard from which Apple changed the face of consumer electronics forever.

It all started in 1998 with the launch of the original iMac, an attention-grabbing computer with translucent plastic, bright coloured details. It was nothing like any previous mainstream computer, and people loved it. Then, in 2007, came the first iPhone.

People around the world camped outside shops overnight to be at the front of the queue for this new, gorgeous, trailblazingly disruptive piece of tech. The frenzy was palpable, and justified; the iPhone lived up to the hype, and fandom and advocacy were sky-high.

What was it about this product that changed the game? With the iPhone, Apple created a whole new category, giving customers something they didn't even know they wanted, but found they couldn't do without.

Something that swapped a physical keyboard for a touchscreen, and packaged all the digital music systems, the internet, email, cameras, phones, handheld gaming devices, personal organisers, and satellite navigation systems into a single, beautifully elegant device. The iPhone is a brilliant example of how different wins, especially when it comes to **product**. By the time it launched, the other Ps were also more in line.

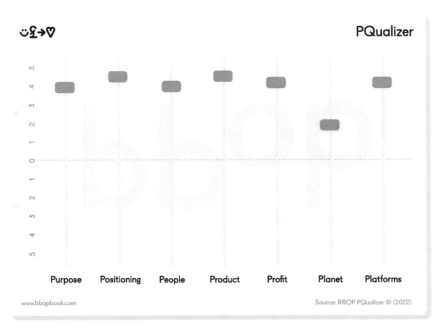

Apple PQualizer - 2007

The iPhone embodied Apple's **purpose**: *'To make a contribution to the world by making tools for the mind that advance humankind.'*

People inside and outside of the business were invigorated by the innovation, demand and impact.

Apple continued to build on their knowledge about how best to leverage their **platforms** by opening retail locations and expanding their 'i' range into cloud and operating system services. It's no secret that **profit** grew rapidly – from just under $2 billion to almost $3.5 billion in 2007 – and has continued to grow year on year ever since.

In terms of **planet**, Apple had a lot of ground to make up. They tackled it head-on, publishing a document that set out the areas where they were performing well, and their plans for those they needed to improve. They succeeded.

As the graph on the following page shows, Apple continued to increase the percentage of recycled materials used year on year.

This trend has continued. By 2021:

→ 59% of all aluminium Apple shipped came from recycled sources

→ Since 2015, Apple has reduced plastic in its packaging by 75% (now accounting for just 4% of all of its packaging)

→ 45% of materials used are certified rare earth materials –

- 30% recycled tin
- 13% certified recycled cobalt
- Certified recycled gold .

WEIGHT RECYCLED AS % OF PAST SALES

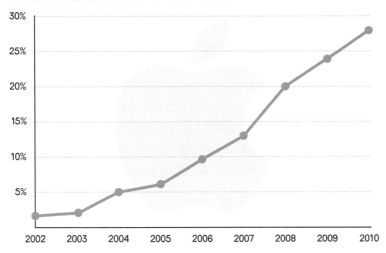

Apple's transformation from struggling tech-corp to world-leading product guru took less than a decade. While the company has its critics, there's no question that it has changed the way we all use technology, forever.

Who else is getting product right?

Queueing to deposit money or pay bills at a bank was never a highlight of anyone's day, especially when they were only open when most people were at work. So when challenger banks like **Monzo**, **Revolut**, **N26** and **Starling** reinvented the banking product, people flocked.

These upstart banks took a digital-first approach, replacing branch and call centre functions with elegant digital tools which put the bank into the customer's pocket. It's an approach that is driving product innovation, and breaking and creating new markets, in sectors such as television (Netflix trumping Blockbuster video) and photography (Instagram eclipsing Kodak).

Luxury travel company, Six Senses are another brand who have got product right. On the face of it, **Six Senses** simply offer luxury travel resorts and spas. But they've redefined what luxury means, creating a product that stands out in a fiercely competitive market.

Luxury for Six Senses is centred around *'The space to reconnect with yourself'*. Resorts are designed to allow guests to go everywhere barefoot, with bicycles provided to get around on. Star-gazing sessions are organised, and mobile phones are locked away. Their focus on sustainability, and determination to be a force for good, extends to reinvesting in local communities and programmes.

2. The impact of getting it wrong

Not all smartphone manufacturers have Apple's post-1997 product skills. Take Samsung, which in 2016 was trying to wrestle the workaholic market from Apple's grasp by making bigger screens. But their desire to do so at speed, against a background of fierce cost management, led to disaster.

Within weeks of the launch of the new Note 7 phone, reports emerged of them setting on fire. It transpired that some factories had crammed batteries into too-small cases, causing them to crimp and malfunction.

In their haste to compete, Samsung had created a phone which could explode in your pocket; hardly a USP. After replacements and recalls, they lost $26 billion on the stock market.

In short

Product is at the heart of your business. It has to be more than good; it has to be exceptional. Get that right, and you put slack into the system, creating space for the other Ps to improve too.

"Every activity that is not aligned with your purpose is a waste of resources."

Michael Kouly

Markets change, but human behaviour doesn't. So make things that people need, and connect the positioning to what they want. Do so with care and consideration, a focus on solving their problems, and a commitment to having a positive impact on the world.

That sometimes means being brave; it often means doing what others aren't. And it always means having your purpose built in.

How Waze used 100 people to design the perfect product

A brilliant example of how having your customers (or potential customers) in the room changes everything, is Waze, a traffic and navigation app co-founded by Uri Levine in 2007.

Levine is an Israeli entrepreneur, living in the highly congested city of Tel Aviv, whose golden rule is *'fall in love with the problem, not the solution.'* He and his colleagues loathed the amount of time they spent in traffic but were aware that creating something more innovative than existing sat-nav systems would be tricky, due to the cost and complexity of licensing the necessary mapping data.

Following his own advice, Levine set out to understand the perception of the problem. He spoke with 100 people, not about how to solve the problem of traffic jams, but instead to understand how others experienced it. This took some time, but it was time well spent.

What Levine learned from his 100 people was that the missing ingredient was real-time data. The existing systems were using mapping and traffic data from the big licensing providers, but this wasn't agile enough to re-route people's journeys in enough time to avoid them getting stuck.

Having dug deep into the problem, Levine and his colleagues were able to develop a solution, which become Waze. This used the speed, direction and positioning data of users to create a real-time map of both road networks and traffic density.

The technology behind it is incredibly clever, and we don't have space to explain it all here. But to summarise, it operates on a crowdsourcing basis, noting that, for example, if several cars start to slow down significantly on a road, you can assume that there's something out there that might be causing a traffic jam, and re-route other users proactively.

Customers loved Waze, and Google agreed; they bought it for $966 million in 2013. There are some clear lessons we can all learn from Levine's people-focused approach to product:

→ Look at where the market is and build for that, rather than for a market that you're predicting will exist.

→ Fall in love with the problem, not the solution.

→ Speak to 100 people you don't know, who aren't like you, about how they experience the problem. Even if you have a solution in mind, don't mention it; your role is to listen.

→ Then use what you learn to understand the emotion which is driving people's needs and wants.

We'll explore these principles, and more, as you read on.

4.2 Score your Product

SCORE YOUR ORGANISATION FOR
POSITIONING USING THE BBOP PQUALIZER

How confident are you in your product & service market fit and adoption?

When you consider what you're offering, how do you score?

5	Your products and services align beautifully with your positioning, are strongly priced and a good market fit, driving high confidence amongst current and potential customers.
3	Confidence is high in some product/service areas, with work to be done on optimisation.
1	Initial product definition and innovation processes are in place, but more work is required to build consumer confidence.
0	No clarity around product, leading to a scattergun approach to what you offer.
-1	An over-reliance on one product or service.
-3	Minimal innovation and a lack of process in place to support the development of products and services.
-5	Your products and services are out of date, commoditised or selling at a loss.

4.3 Product in Action

All BBOPs should aim to create compelling products and services, of exceptional quality, which answer people's needs and improve their lives. As the Waze story shows, understanding the problem that you're trying to solve, before you attempt to solve it, is central to doing this well.

We will now lay out the five steps that will help you purposefully design and build a product or service that your target audience will love, buy, and recommend.

Five steps to shift your approach to product

1. Build emotional design into your product development

2. Understand the problem your product will solve

3. Know your market

4. Harmonise product and planet

5. Remember that different wins

1. Build emotional design into your product development

Field of Dreams is a smashing film, but its core premise, *'If you build it, they will come',* is unfortunately just not true when it comes to product design.

Product is about the way you make someone feel. It's not just the thing you are selling; it's the whole experience that your customer enjoys. If a competitor is offering an inferior product, but a better experience, their sales may well outstrip yours. As Steve Jobs explains:

'People DO judge a book by its cover. We may have the best product, the highest quality, the most useful software etc... but if we present them in a slipshod manner, they will be perceived as slipshod; if we present them in a creative, professional manner, we will impute the desired qualities.'

How can you make sure your product or service is received in the way it deserves? The answer is to build emotional design, as well as physical design, into your product development process – not just within the product or service you are building, but within every interaction; the relationship between product and positioning is a close one, and critical to the product's ultimate success.

There are three core ingredients you need to consider when exploring emotional design, based on the cognitive responses that you're seeking to influence:

1. **Visceral:** A user's gut reaction, their first impression. The strength of this reaction is shown by the number of people who will watch YouTubers unboxing new products.

2. **Behavioural:** A user's subconscious evaluation of how your product will help them achieve their goals. They need to feel that they're in control, with minimum effort required, so the easier you can make this, the better.

3. **Reflective:** A user's considered personal judgement, based on the product's benefits to them, value for money and performance.

All three are important, but it's when your product nails the reflective response that the magic happens. It means your users will keep using it, and so keep buying it; they may even become advocates and do your marketing for you.

EMOTIONAL DESIGN

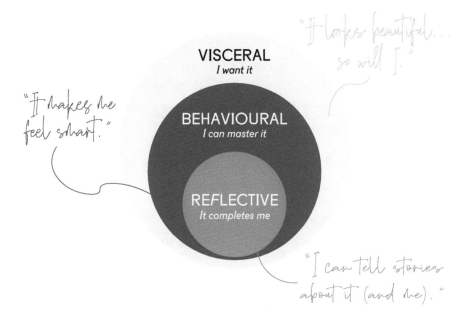

2. Understand the problem your product will solve

Comedian Steve Martin's advice to aspiring entertainers is *'Be so good they can't ignore you'*. And Cal Newport, who used this phrase as the title of his best-selling book, applies it to the business world. He believes that if you focus on being so good at what you do that people are in desperate need of what you offer, you can't fail.

Now, the chances are, you think you've got an idea for a great product or service; why else would you bother? But it is your customers, not you, who will decide how good it is. The way to make it so good that they can't ignore it is to give them what they want and need.

To start with, that means being confident that the market is ready for your idea. If it is so radical that it will only be wanted or needed in five, ten or twenty years, it's probably too early to throw all your efforts behind it. The risk of getting it wrong will be much lower if you wait for the market to mature.

It also means deciphering what their wants and needs actually are. This is harder than you'd expect, because it may be different from what they say, particularly if what you're offering is radically different from what currently exists. After all, if Henry Ford had asked people what they wanted, they would have said a faster horse, not a car.

Luckily, in today's digital world, there are a number of ways to get clues about what people really want. For example:

→ Use Google Trends to see what people are searching for, and how volumes around searches are changing over time: https://trends. google.com/trends/

→ Build sophisticated searches on Twitter to find your potential customers, and understand what they're talking about, in the context of your product: https://twitter.com/search-advanced

→ Get early insights by putting together a landing page that sells the proposition of your product, and gives potential customers the option to buy online. Drive traffic to the landing page through targeted, paid ads. Then look at the conversion rates to understand whether your proposed product will fly.

If the product isn't ready, you can offer a pre-ordering facility, with a discount that rewards potential customers for being prepared to wait.

Another frequently used route to a great idea is to scratch your own itch – that is, to solve a problem you are experiencing. Like our old friend Levine, who created Waze to overcome his frustration about being stuck in traffic.

But remember, we all have our own biases; so while your own opinion might be a good starting point, you should back it up with insights from a wider group, just as Levine did.

3. Know your market

When designing or refining a product, the default behaviour is often to build for the widest audience possible. But while the mass market may seem appealing, this isn't the best approach.

Instead, consider the concept of 1,000 true fans, suggested by Kevin Kelly, polymath and founding editor of *Wired* magazine. This suggests that to build a business, or a movement, you only need to focus on your first 1,000 customers or followers; people who truly love what you offer because they want it so much.

Geoffrey A. Moore takes this concept further in his book, *Crossing the Chasm*. He notes that most products in an emerging market are built for the majority of potential customers, and argues that it's better to build products for the groups who sit on the other side of the chasm.

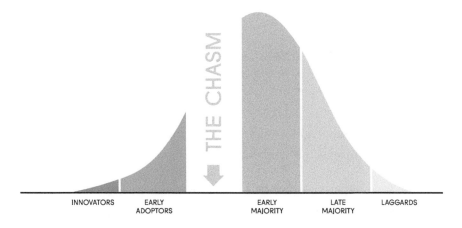

Source: "Crossing The Chasm" Geoffrey Moore (Harper Business, 2014)

Moore's point is that the innovators and early adopters are so passionate about your purpose that they'll forgive the fact that your product is a bit rough around the edges and will go on the journey with you. If you listen to them, and include their views in your product's evolution, they'll help you cross the chasm to a much bigger market.

Some things to consider:

→ Product design isn't a one-off process; successful products evolve as the culture changes, and the market matures. Embrace this principle in your product design, and build in cycles where you iterate, launch, learn, and repeat.

→ For every new iteration, assemble a diverse team, including potential customers, to design a minimum viable product (MVP). Then shift your focus to getting that product used (and paid for) by real customers, and use their insights to guide your next iteration.

→ It's a well-established business principle that 'perfect' is the enemy of 'good enough'; if you spend too long chasing perfection, the market may have moved on.

However brilliant a product may be, if there isn't a market, it won't sell.

4. Harmonise product and planet

When product and planet are out of balance, all the other Ps suffer. Profit isn't sustainable; your people won't become advocates; your purpose and positioning will seem hollow. If you dial up your platforms for scalability, the negative impact will be even bigger.

It's our (possibly optimistic) belief that, over time, companies will have little choice but to be more ethical. Technology will play a part; banks such as NatWest in the UK are already showing individual carbon footprint measures within their banking apps, and not-for-profit Ecologi is developing a product, Ecologi Zero, which shows each business their carbon emissions across their supply chain.

Stricter laws and legislation will, we hope, come soon; the power of legislation can be seen right now in Norway, where heavier taxation on petrol cars has led to their sales being eclipsed by electric rivals.

But in the meantime, it's up to BBOPs to champion the value of considering the planet while developing new products. While that's clearly the right thing to do, it will also, given the paucity of many organisations' green credentials, give your business an edge.

Follow these four core principles to harmonise your product and planet strategies:

→ **Leave no trace.** If you can't avoid impacting the planet, build or seek out a solution. For example, if you need physical packaging for your product, eco-friendly solutions are out there; the global biodegradable packaging market is growing at a rate of 6.35% per year. This may cost more and have a knock-on effect on your prices; but even if this reduces your market (and therefore your profit) in the short term, you should still embrace it for the long term.

→ **Build for a lifetime, not landfill**, and say no to planned obsolescence. Patagonia offer an *'ironclad guarantee'* which entitles all customers to returns, replacements, refunds or repairs, whenever they need them.

→ **Embrace a circular economy model** where products are designed to be passed on; after all, one person's waste is another's treasure. Like Redwood Materials, co-founded by JB Straubel, who also co-founded Tesla. They extract sustainable materials, including nickel, cobalt and lithium, from old smartphones, power tools and scooter batteries, and put them back into the supply chain.

→ **Pay it forward.** As a BBOP, you should seek opportunities to take this circular economy model further, using company resources to improve your local community and the lives of those who live and work within it.

5. Remember that different wins

It's an easy mistake to make, but many companies, when developing or enhancing their products, tend to avoid being different. It feels safer, perhaps, to use existing products as a guide, and follow their norms.

However, as we saw in the Waze example, focusing on the problem and not the solution can result in something fundamentally different from existing products in your category. We'd argue that different isn't bad, wrong or risky; if you follow the process, different wins.

Zappos and the art of legendary customer service

A great example of this is Zappos, who started selling footwear online in 1998, just as people were getting comfortable with the concept of e-commerce.

The problem, which everyone involved in the early days of internet shopping was grappling with, was that the convenience of selling online came with some big logistical costs. With shoes, in particular, returns were high, due to non-standardised sizing and fit, which required a huge customer service operation.

At the time, shoes were a $40 billion market in the U.S. and 5% of them were already sold by mail order. Zappos founder, Nick Swinmurn, decided to differentiate his company by ditching advertising and investing the money in exceptional customer service, so their customers would do the marketing for them through word of mouth. As Tony Hsieh, Zappos CEO, explained:

'To WOW, you must differentiate yourself, which means do something a little unconventional and innovative. You must do something that's above and beyond what's expected. And whatever you do must have an emotional impact on the receiver.'

Perhaps the most famous example of this legendary customer service in action is the time that a best man contacted Zappos because he'd lost his shoes. They couriered him a replacement pair overnight, at no cost, and upgraded his account to VIP. Zappos embraced different, and used it to build an incredible BBOP.

Of course, it's possible to be different in a less dramatic way, and evolve, rather than totally rethink. For example, in response to more and more marketing services being brought in house, Oliver Agency built the world's first company that designs, builds and runs bespoke in-house agencies and marketing ecosystems for brands. While other agencies were resisting the change, Oliver Agency embraced it – and reaped the rewards.

In short

If you build for everyone, you're building for no one. So start by understanding what problem your product could solve. Then focus on the early adopters and design and iterate the product with them, remembering to incorporate emotional design principles as well as physical ones.

As you go through the process, make it a priority to create something that is net positive for the planet; it will help you differentiate from your competitors and inspire advocacy, as well as contribute to the greater good.

Design your products to be different; not for the sake of it, but because it is often what customers really want and need. So find your different, fully embrace it and embed it into your product.

4.4 Product: jump off points

Questions to spur you into action

→ What's the problem that your product could solve?

→ How do your customers experience that problem?

→ How do they currently feel, and what do they want to feel?

→ Is your product design process iterative?

→ Are you focusing on good enough, or perfect products?

→ Would you prefer to have 10,000 people who are interested in your product, or 100 paying customers?

→ What market are you building for, and how mature is it?

→ How close are you to a net-positive product proposition? What do you need to change to get there?

→ How is your product different, and how confidently are you embodying this in your product design and positioning?

NOW RE-SCORE YOURSELF ON THE PQUALIZER

5 PROFIT

A note about profit

While the widely accepted definition of profit is the difference between the amount earned and the amount spent on operating and producing, we believe this is both narrow and shallow. We also think it seriously limits what a business can achieve.

The reality is, there are many other historic and progressive legal structures in business that are not solely focused on driving a financial profit. Charities, not-for-profits and community interest companies are just three examples. And businesses can be sustained through a range of financial sources, such as fundraising, donations, investment, government grants and self-generated profit.

For a Better Business On Purpose, what's critical is having sustained and sustainable finance which will allow you to achieve your goals. And the most tried and tested method of achieving this is to make a profit that can be reinvested. So, for the purpose of this book, profit is not purely money to be taken out of your business, but the fuel that funds the progression, innovation and sustainable future of your organisation.

Profit may not be immediate, or the main driver of financial success, in some organisations. Two examples would be start-ups, kickstarted by external investment, or more mature companies where external investment is sought to grow or relocate.

Any actual profits earned are funnelled back to business owners, who then have the choice to pocket the cash, or reinvest it back into the business. As a BBOP, this very decision will define the sustainability of your dream.

5.1 Profit: From maximising profit to maximising your profit's potential

Make profit with pride and use it to fuel your purpose. Profit is not a dirty word; every BBOP needs a strong and sustainable commercial model to thrive. So while it's not the only reason to exist, it matters; and being good at creating it is nothing to be ashamed of.

What we'll explore:

1. What it looks like when you get profit right

2. The impact of getting it wrong

Heads up: Why it's worth being purposeful about profit

Profit is essential for any BBOP. It allows the organisation to be self-sustaining and provides the capital it needs to innovate and become a force for good. Simply put, no profit, no progress.

We see business wealth as much more than just financial security; it can also be social, cultural, intellectual or environmental. And businesses have the potential to both create and destroy it in all its forms.

However, for too long, too many businesses have been looking at profit from the wrong perspective, with financial maximisation seen as the primary driver. This is a problem, because pursuing financial wealth at the expense of all the other Ps is not a sustainable game to play.

A BBOP takes the alternative view, seeing profit as a powerful means to an end, and a way to deliver against purpose, rather than the ultimate goal.

To echo the words of leading UK economist Sir John Kay, *'Profit is no more the purpose of business than breathing is the purpose of living.'*

1. What it looks like when you get profit right

Sara Blakely, founder of Spanx and one of TIME's 100 Most Influential People, is a one-woman case study of how to go from running a start-up to becoming a billionaire, reinvesting profit all the way.

Originally a door-to-door fax machine seller, she had a dream of selling something she'd created and actually cared about. And her dream came to life one day when she was trying to work out what to wear to a party. As she noted in an interview with CNBC in 2012:

'In the hope of looking better in my fitted white pants, I cut the feet out of a pair of pantyhose and substituted them for my underwear. This allowed me to benefit from the slimming effects of the pantyhose's "control top" … the moment I saw how good my butt looked, I was like, "Thank you, God, this is my opportunity!"'

The result was Spanx, a unique type of body shapewear that is thin, comfortable and invisible under clothes. And the trajectory of the company behind it is dizzying:

→ **1998:** Blakely starts Spanx with $5,000 in savings, bootstrapping the growth of the company on product sales. Large purchase orders come rushing in.

→ **1999:** Spanx's first-year revenue tops $4,000,000, with no follow-on funding. Having self-funded the business from the beginning, Sara is the sole owner.

→ **1999:** Blakely succeeds in getting Neiman Marcus (a high-end US department store) to stock her products.

→ **2000:** Oprah names Spanx her favourite product of the year, causing sales to exponentially take off. Sales hit $10,000,000 in revenue.

→ **2001:** Spanx is featured on QVC and sells more than 8,000 units in under six minutes.

→ **2013:** Blakely sells a majority share in Spanx – now valued at an estimated $1.2 billion – to global investment firm Blackstone. Aged just 41, she becomes the youngest self-made female billionaire.

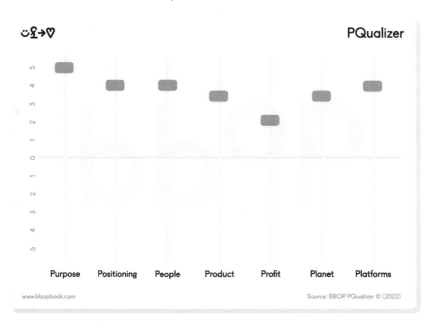

Now, we're not saying that profit was Sara's only driver. As you can see in our interpretation of the PQualizer for Spanx at the time of writing, while **profit** is in a strong, positive position, it's not dominating. And critically, all the Ps are in balance.

Spanx's **purpose**, *Elevating Women*, rings as true today as it did when the company launched. The company website expands it as follows:

'Spanx® is a brand for women, by women. We obsess about comfort, deliver results and ensure you look as good as you feel. We think forward and give back. We believe women can do anything. And together, we believe we will make the world a better place... one butt at a time!'

The company's focus on **people** played a huge part in what makes her **product** so wildly popular, and is still at the heart of production today. Before Spanx, all sizes of pantyhose were designed with the same waistband, for cost-cutting reasons. This made them so uncomfortable that some customers were unable to breathe (a pretty basic fail). Spanx broke the nylon mould, creating different-sized waistbands across the range, and testing them on women of all shapes and sizes.

As a result, Spanx's **positioning** as the product to *'help women feel great about themselves and their potential'* is authentic and believable. And this help is being rolled out on a global scale. The company trades in over 50 countries worldwide, and their **planet**-wide focus includes the creation of the Sara Blakely Foundation, which has donated millions to charities such as the Malala Fund and Vital Voices, focused on empowering underserved women and girls.

Despite her huge success, Blakely isn't running away with the proceeds. Instead, she's chosen to sign the Melinda French Gates, Bill Gates and Warren Buffett Giving Pledge, which commits her to giving at least half of her wealth to charity. Overall, then, Spanx is a clear example of creating positive impact, both within and outside of a business.

2. The impact of getting it wrong

Reinvesting profit to grow sustainably, and give generously, elevates the business itself and the world beyond it. Unfortunately, this combination of purposeful reinvestment and philanthropy is not in any sense the norm, with too many companies taking the opposite approach.

Take We Work, for example, which we explored in Shift 2; it's no exaggeration to say that Adam Neumann and Sara Blakely sit at opposing ends of the purposeful profit spectrum. Or take Meta, the recently renamed parent company of Facebook, Instagram and WhatsApp, whose $1 trillion success is somewhat tarnished by questions around how they acquire and apply their profit.

There are concerns about the purpose, intent and anti-trust status of the business, as well as their controversial approach to paying tax. Facebook, in particular, has been accused of damaging young people's mental health, enabling election rigging and facilitating terrorist activity.

These concerns led civil rights groups to target Facebook and Instagram's advertising revenue with the 2020 #StopHateForProfit campaign, which encouraged an advertising boycott of the platforms. As our old friends Patagonia explained, *'They spread hate speech and misinformation about climate change and our democracy'*, adding, *'We encourage other businesses to join us in pushing Facebook to prioritise people and planet over profit.'*

All of which may have played a part in their decision to rename and reframe the business under the Meta umbrella. Only time will tell if this is enough to detoxify their brand; we suspect a substantial rethink of their approach to profit would be a better place to start.

When business leaders treat profit as the fuel that will share their purpose with the world, rather than a goal in its own right, it can be rewarding for everyone involved. When profit takes priority over all other aspects of the business, everyone loses.

As a leader who is seeking to become a force for good, your approach should mirror the former. Are you succeeding?

5.2 Score your Profit

 SCORE YOUR ORGANISATION FOR
POSITIONING USING THE BBOP PQUALIZER

Is your business commercially robust, generating profit to be able to invest and grow?

How would you score? Would your finance director agree?

5	Commercially strong and confident for the future, able to invest and grow.
3	Delivering sustainable profit with a relatively low margin.
1	In profit, not yet sustainable or consistent enough to continue to innovate.
0	Just about breaking even.
-1	Struggling to break even, with a lack of handle on financial detail.
-3	Unable to forecast a profit.
-5	Making a sustained loss, with no recovery or profitability plan.

5.3 Profit in Action

We noted that profit is not a dirty word, and that a healthy bottom line is the fuel that allows BBOPs to operate and innovate, in a purposeful way. Next, we will explore the cyclical nature of profit, and set out the six essential finance principles that will act as strong, sustainable foundations for your business:

Six steps to shift your approach to profit

1. Seek value beyond profit

2. Build on the 7Ps to broaden your definition of value

3. Master the language of finance

4. Make tax schemes work for you

5. Turn debt into an asset

6. Reinvest for good

1. Seek value beyond profit

In 1994, John Elkington, founder of consulting company SustainAbility, summed up a new way to quantify value with a simple concept: the triple bottom line. His view was that businesses should measure their performance in relation to people, planet and profit, rather than profit alone.

Fast forward almost three decades and this concept is finally getting the traction it deserves. Businesses are recognising that the pursuit of profit alone is no longer sustainable. There's also a growing focus on, and investment in, companies' ESG (environmental, social and governance) credentials.

"Profits happen when you do everything else right."

Yvon Chouinard

And customers are increasingly interested in supporting companies that align with their beliefs, as Zeno's 2020 Strength of Purpose research showed:

*After evaluating over 75 brands, the research found that global consumers are **four to six times more likely to trust, buy, champion and protect** those companies with a strong purpose over those with a weaker one. (Zeno, 17 June 2020)*

As Alison DaSilva, the Purpose and Impact Zeno Group MD, explained in a *Forbes* interview, there is a clear sense that the single-minded pursuit of profit is no longer right:

'Globally, 94% of consumers said it is important that the companies they engage with have a **strong purpose**, and 83% said companies should **only** earn a profit if they also deliver a **positive impact**.'

In today's world, it makes financial sense for all businesses to track social and environmental performance, as well as commercial achievements. And for purpose-driven businesses, this approach should be baked in.

2. Build on the 7Ps to broaden your definition of value

However, for those of us within the BBOP movement, the triple bottom line is just a starting point. Yes, it moves away from having financial maximisation as the only goal, and incorporates three of the 7Ps – profit, people and planet. But because it ignores the other four, its impact is limited.

And interestingly, we're not the only ones who feel this way; in 2020, Elkington took the bold decision to 'recall' the concept of the triple bottom line, believing it doesn't go far enough.

We believe that the best way to maximize value, and broaden the concept of what value means, is by aligning the 7Ps. This leads to a more sustainable approach in which **profits** are driven by a clear **purpose**, strong **positioning**, engaged and enthusiastic **people**, and delivering much-wanted **products** and services, through effective **platforms,** to scale and grow a business that offers a positive contribution to our **planet**.

Committing to this 7-way alignment empowers founders to make decisions based on keeping all the different elements healthy and balanced. The result is a business that acts as a force for good in the world, using its profits as fuel to create a positive impact on all stakeholders. And that's far more fulfilling than pure financial maximisation for shareholders alone.

3. Master the language of finance

Warren Buffett, who's had a decent amount of corporate success, believes that *'accounting is the language of business'*. And he's right; cashflow, profit and loss are the essential foundations on which any successful business is built.

So if you want to maximise the positive impact of your BBOP, you need to have a clear and complete understanding of the different elements that feed into your accounting structure. With apologies to any finance directors that might be reading this, here's a friendly reminder of the most important ones:

→ **Cashflow.** Cash is king, so treat it like royalty. It is more liquid than other forms of investment tools such as stocks or bonds, and you can't make non-credit purchases, settle debts or pay dividends to shareholders without it. The ability to generate and use cash well is a sign of a healthy business.

→ **Profit.** This is the easiest thing to measure; it's the revenue a business earns, minus expenses, and is usually calculated in one of two ways:

→ **Gross profit** – the difference between your sales and the direct cost of making those sales isn't pure profit, so don't take it out of the business at this point.

- **Net profit** – the total gross profit, minus all business expenses; you can distribute this, or ideally, reinvest it.

- **Profit and loss.** Also known as the P&L, the income statement or the management accounts; this is essentially a listing of sales and expenses. If you're making a profit, that's great, keep leveraging it. If you're making a loss, make changes, quickly.

→ **Revenue.** The amount your business earns before expenses, tax and other deductions.

→ **Margin.** The difference between revenue and expenses. Every industry has its own benchmarks: in restaurants, it's usually around 2-6%; in the automotive industry it's rarely in double-digits. In software, it's not unusual to see margins at an eye-watering 70%.

→ **Assets.** Everything your business owns that has a financial value, from cash to computers, inventory to IP, furniture to franchises.

→ **Liability.** Your financial commitments or monies owed by you.

→ **Balance sheet.** A list of all your assets and liabilities, demonstrating your net asset position. The higher your net assets, the stronger your business; the lower your net assets, the weaker your position.

→ **Break-even.** The point at which sales revenue in = expenses out. When you're starting out, it pays to get here as quickly as possible.

→ **Financial model.** A clear budget and forecast that will underpin the decisions you make around hiring, investing and growing.

→ **Investing.** Financial outlay that requires a return. Not to be confused with spending, which is a financial outlay that **doesn't** require a return. Investing can further drive profit; spending won't.

Once you master the language, there are several elements you need to have a really clear handle on:

→ Your cashflow model

→ Your P&L and balance sheet

→ Gross and net profit calculations

→ Your break-even point

You may be asking yourself, isn't all this for FDs to worry about? Why do I need to know it too? And the answer is, because you need to be able to constantly recalibrate your business to ensure that it's fulfilling your purpose. Understanding these core principles will help you make good decisions about your business, which will keep it well fuelled and increase its positive impact.

Two final points. Don't assume everyone has financial competence; teach it across the organisation. And understand that profit alone doesn't motivate everyone, so make sure you show what it does, not just what it is.

4. Make tax schemes work for you

There are a range of tax incentive schemes out there that can help you grow your business – you just need to know where to find them. Here are a few ideas to get you started:

→ **R&D Tax Credits** are offered in the UK, US & Canada, Japan, Spain and Hungary at a central and subnational (regional) level, to support businesses to drive innovation in science and technology.

→ In the UK, the incentives are particularly enticing. If you can advance the field you are working in (not just your business) and you fit the rules around staffing and turnover levels, you may be able to deduct an extra 130% of qualifying costs from your yearly profit. Added to the normal 100% deduction, that's a total of 230% off your corporation tax.

→ In the US, if you need to spend money rehabilitating dilapidated buildings to make a project financially viable, you may qualify for **Low-Income Tax Credits** (from the Department of Housing and Urban Development) and a **Historic Preservation Tax Credit** (from the National Park Service).

→ Many countries offer incentives to **develop, maintain and promote a country's film industry**. In Australia, there is a 16.5% tax rebate for the production of large budget film and tv projects, with a 30% rebate for post-production. France offers a 30% tax rebate for international productions, and Poland a subsidy of up to 50% of the film budget.

These are just three examples amongst many, so it's worth investing the time to find schemes that match your business, and make them work for you. If you're not confident about navigating this alone, invest in a commercial person with a deep understanding of tax law, who is both fluent in your industry and aligned with your values. It will pay dividends. Literally.

5. Turn debt into an asset

It's almost impossible to build a truly scalable business without incurring any debt. However, it's a tough subject, and one that can cause real difficulty. Co-founders and leaders often have different attitudes to risk, based on their past experiences, and if a debt decision has to be personally guaranteed, it can be immensely difficult to navigate.

Here are some of the different ways that you may encounter debt within your business:

→ You may want to be strategic about how you set up your creditor days and debtor days. Don't pay out before you are paid, otherwise you'll end up robbing Peter to pay Paul.

→ You may be using your tax payments to invest in growth before the tax bill arrives (as tax bills are always in arrears).

→ You may have taken up a government-backed loan that is affordable to finance. For example, in the UK, CBILS loans were provided to help businesses to stay afloat through the Covid-19 storm.

→ You may feel your business would benefit from an injection of money from a venture capitalist or bank (ideally one that is aligned to your purpose, or seeking more than just pure financial return).

The fact is debt, like profit, isn't a dirty word. And if you've got a business that's starting to look good, money in the form of debt or investment will likely find you. So the important thing is to have the right mindset, and see it as an opportunity, rather than a threat.

If you can afford to access cheap money that comes with the right investment, on the right terms, it's worth considering; it can be used as fuel for growth. Invest it, rather than spending it on stuff you don't need; and if you don't use it, give it back.

You'll need to take into account your leadership team's attitude to debt, your risk profile, and the long-term impact of any debt you take on. But don't avoid it just because it's something you're not comfortable with right now, or have had a bad experience with in the past. Used carefully, and purposefully, debt is something every business could potentially use to its advantage.

6. Reinvest for good

As we work to widen the impact of the BBOP movement, we're seeking out leaders and founders with soul; people who have taken a deliberate decision to pursue meaningful goals over pure financial gains alone.

We are lucky enough to live in an era where there are many potential allies for this journey. The globally galvanising team behind B Corp (who we cover in more depth in the next chapter) and the inspiring crew at 1% for the Planet, are two particularly strong leaders in this field.

1% for the Planet encourage responsible business to create a healthier world by giving back to environmentally focused charities and not-for-profits. The result is an incredible network of empowered, aligned organisations who are supporting our planet by donating 1% of their sales each year.

All those 1% donations add up; as of May 2022, 1% for the Planet had given back almost $350m in a targeted, impactful way. As they like to say, *'We can do more together than we can do alone'*.

So whether you choose to reinvest your profits within your own business, or by donating to an ecosystem with a wider reach, there are plenty of ways to pursue your meaningful goals.

In short

Don't be apologetic about driving hard to generate profit. It's the fuel for your business and, providing it is aligned with your purpose and in balance with your business drivers, will be a force for good.

Change your perspective of profit from a one-dimensional business outcome to a multi-dimensional driving force. And make sure you understand the nuts and bolts of how to make it work for your business.

This will allow you to escalate your **purpose**, boost your **positioning**, intensify the engagement of your **people**, improve your **products** and leave a **positive** legacy for generations to come.

5.4 Profit: jump off points

Questions to spur you into action

→ Do you have a strong commercial grip on your organisation?

→ Are you tracking your metrics over time – weekly, quarterly and annually?

→ Is your profit fuelling progress at every level of your business? How?

→ Are you using debt to fuel your purpose – or is it dragging you back?

→ Do you have a clear spending and investment strategy?

→ Are you taking advantage of tax breaks and other external support?

→ Is your profit amplifying your impact, through your own business or in partnership with allies?

NOW RE-SCORE YOURSELF ON THE PQUALIZER

6 PLANET

6.1 Planet: From taking out to putting back in

Make sure your business delivers on environmental, ethical and community issues, within the way you do business, as well as through your services and products. As David Hieatt puts it in his own Do Manifesto: *'If you are going to make change happen, make it good. The planet needs as many friends as it can get.'*

What we'll explore

1. What it looks like when you get planet right

2. The impact of getting it wrong

Heads up: Why being purposeful about our planet matters

Looking after the planet, and the communities who live on it, is arguably the most important job that any of us have to do. Although the fact that you're reading this book suggests you're probably on the same page as us regarding this issue, it never hurts to have a reminder of how serious things are.

As the graph on the right shows, global emissions have risen dramatically over the last 120 years – and exponentially in the last 70. If we are to hit the United Nations COP26 2050 Net Zero goal, which in turn will help reduce global heating to 1.5^0, they will need to fall even faster than they have risen. If we don't, the impact on the planet and its inhabitants will be catastrophic.

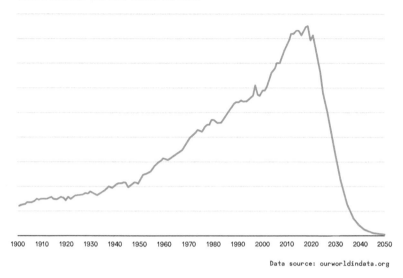

HISTORIC GLOBAL GHG EMISSIONS
AND PATHWAY TO NET ZERO IN 2050

1900 1910 1920 1930 1940 1950 1960 1970 1980 1990 2000 2010 2020 2030 2040 2050

Data source: ourworldindata.org

It's a huge challenge, and one that will require global collaboration as well as individual action. But as a business leader, you have a unique opportunity to contribute by driving positive behavioural change on a wider scale, across your teams and customers, and your products and processes.

On a less altruistic note, you'll also benefit from the growing global movement for greater good. Increasingly, customer buying decisions are influenced by the ethical impact of a business, on the environment (local and global) and their community. What's good for the planet can be good for your bottom line, too.

1. What it looks like when you get planet right

You may be surprised to learn that a company which produces 19 million pieces of plastic every year is considered a green gamechanger. Yet there's no question that LEGO is building a solid set of ethical credentials, due to their planet-focused approach.

The globally renowned, family-owned Danish firm have set aside $400 million and a team of 100 people to go green by 2030. And they're prepared to be held to account, too, publicly stating their ambition on Twitter:

'Our mission is to inspire and develop the builders of tomorrow. We do this through play which gives children skills to imagine and build a brighter future. And we do it through working hard to have a positive impact on the environment and our communities.'

A central part of this commitment is LEGO's pledge to stop using oil-based plastics in their toys. After decades of relying on fossil fuels, they have invested time and money into using recycled plastic bottles to make their bricks (their long-term aim is to make them entirely from sustainable materials such as sugar cane) and they have stopped using plastic bags in their packaging.

This **purpose-led** determination to limit harm to the **planet** through the way they produce their **products** explains the scores we would give LEGO for these three elements on our PQualizer. And their planet-friendly focus is weaved into the other Ps, which also have high ratings.

Whilst known for making a healthy **profit** – which was up 19% in 2020 on the previous year – they bring a green perspective to what they do with it, investing in companies that champion recycling plastic and plastic alternatives.

They are also willing to listen to the young **people** who use their products, and take on board their suggestions for alternatives to plastic. As CEO Niels B. Christiansen said in 2021: *'The feedback we get from our customers is very clear. The younger kids are, the more direct they are with their views on the green transition and sustainability.'*

Lego PQualizer

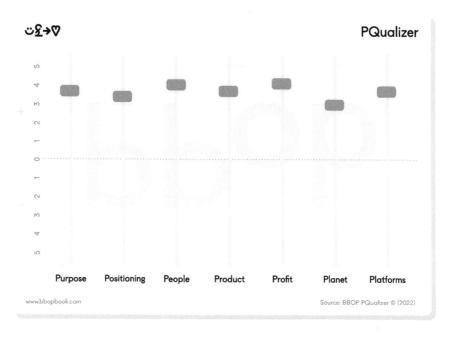

Source: BBOP PQualizer © (2022)

Their ethical **positioning** is underpinned by 12 principles, published clearly on their website, covering issues such as business conduct, employee rights and regulating their suppliers. As a result, they consistently come out on top in *'most reputable company'* and *'company culture'* rankings.

Alongside the development of digital **platforms** that allow LEGO to stay relevant to today's virtually-adept children, they have widened their offering to include box-office-smashing films that champion inclusion and positivity.

For young people, and for their nostalgia-filled parents, there's little doubt that LEGO are predominantly a force for good – and seem determined to continue to be so.

Now, clearly, LEGO is a global business, whose decisions have a global impact. So it's easy to see why you and your smaller business peers might feel powerless in comparison. But every journey is made up of individual steps, and if a large volume of small businesses implement real, ethical changes in the way they are run, visible progress will be made.

Your small-scale agility helps, too; it allows you to make changes, such as switching to an ethical electricity supplier far more swiftly than your larger peers. And when it comes to the planet, time is in short supply.

Who else is getting planet right?

Unlike LEGO, most companies don't have $400 million to invest in research on becoming greener. But that hasn't prevented some excellent organisations from doing their bit for the planet, and for the communities who live on it.

Take **Innocent**, the smoothie supplier. The company buys fruit through the Rainforest Alliance, which works with farmers to conserve biodiversity and protect farmworkers' rights. They have been incorporating recycled plastic into their packaging since 2003 and give 10% of annual profits to charity. Innocent have partnered with The Felix Project, a charity that redistributes surplus food to those in poverty across London.

Then there's **Rabbit Group**, providers of waste management and skip hire services. The company's founders were concerned about landfill but recognised that the UK was 'not geared up for recycling, nor prepared to pay for it'. So they built the UK's first privately funded, biomass Energy Recovery Facility in Lancing, West Sussex. It opened in 2008 and is capable of generating up to 55 megawatts of green energy (enough to power around 3000 average homes for one year) which is sold onto the national grid.

Let's not forget the way UK high-street cobbler **Timpsons** has a direct, positive impact on the communities in which their shops are based. The company has a policy of recruiting recently released prisoners, who might otherwise struggle to make the cut and end up unemployed or, worse, back inside. As a result, ex-offenders now make up 10% of their workforce.

2. The impact of getting it wrong

The flip side of shoppers' willingness to base buying decisions on ethical credentials is their absolute ruthlessness when a company gets it wrong. When brands are caught making planet-wrecking or community-harming decisions, or trying to boost their image through greenwashing, they suffer, financially and reputationally.

Perhaps unsurprisingly, companies that produce or rely on fossil fuels are often the worst offenders. As we noted in the introduction to this section, a notorious example of this is Volkswagen, who engineered and installed computer software that could deliberately mislead car emission testing – and took a massive financial hit as a result.

Similarly, Shell Oil was called out on national television in **Joe Lycett vs The Oil Giant**. Despite running adverts celebrating wind turbines, solar panels and cycling as an alternative mode of transport, the company gave renewable energy projects just 1% of the $116 billion they had available for reinvestment in 2020.

Lycett brought the hypocrisy to life by posing as CEO Ben van Beurden for a spoof advert, during which fake excrement erupted from his mouth every time he tried to speak. Not the kind of publicity they were hoping for.

In short

The demand for ethical brands is on the rise, but it is flanked by a need for authenticity. People are becoming increasingly wise to greenwashing, and it's not enough to talk the talk; you need to walk the walk, too.

As a founder, business owner or leader, you have the power – and the responsibility – to make sure your business is contributing to the global movement for greater good.

From improving the ethical credentials of the products or services you offer to actively helping communities or under-represented individuals, use your BBOP to create impact, and a legacy, that you can be proud of.

6.2 Score your Planet

SCORE YOUR ORGANISATION FOR
POSITIONING USING THE BBOP PQUALIZER

Does your business have a positive impact on our planet and the people who live on it?

How would you score it on environmental and ethical grounds?

5	You are operating as a BBOP, so the more you scale, the more net good you create.
3	Your organisation is having a measurable positive impact on our world.
1	You are working towards being a BBOP.
0	You recognise that you need to take action around environmental issues, but are yet to do so, which may be having an unintentionally negative impact.
-1	You are being negligent about your environmental impact and having a sustained (if unintentional) negative effect on our world.
-3	You know, or suspect, that your organisation is actively causing environmental damage.
-5	Your organisation is causing sustained, potentially irreversible damage to our world.

6.3 Planet in Action

Delivering on environmental, ethical and community issues is mission-critical for any BBOP. We also recognise the negative impact of companies whose short-term, profit-led approach sees them taking out rather than putting back in, and trying to disguise this through greenwashing.

We shall now set out the four steps to developing an ethical business which 'walks the walk' as well as 'talks the talk', putting back in for the planet and the communities who live on it.

Four steps to shift your approach to planet

1. Start change from within

2. Engage your stakeholders

3. Avoid meaningless gestures

4. Do what you can

1. Start change from within

As we noted back in Chapter xx, the growing global movement for greater good means customers are increasingly influenced by the ethical impact of a business on the environment and their community. This is affecting their buying decisions and creating opportunities for companies who are genuinely ethically focused.

However, the system isn't set up to support this change. In her book, *Doughnut Economics: Seven Ways to Think Like a 21st-Century Economist*, Kate Raworth claims that economics is broken, and the world is paying the price. More positively, she also offers a radical re-envisioning of the system into one that meets all our needs, without exhausting the planet.

But until the systems are overhauled, it's up to us all to do what we can. Change comes from within; here's how to get started.

Evaluate your status quo

Begin by understanding what you are taking out from the planet as a company. We'd suggest breaking your business down into the following five areas and considering what ethical improvements you can make.

→ **Energy.** How much energy do you use, and how could you use less? Does your supplier offer renewable energy?

→ **Transport.** How do you move your products around, and how do your team travel to and from work? Could this be improved?

→ **Buildings.** What can you do to make your premises more energy efficient?

→ **Procurement.** What impact do your suppliers and their networks have on the environment and local communities? How do they procure and manufacture their materials? This should cover physical goods and services, including supply logistics and even your pension company.

→ **Waste.** What happens to all the refuse and leftovers from the day-to-day operations of your business?

Helpfully, in his insightful book, *How Bad Are Bananas?*, Mike Berners-Lee has done some of the sums for us.

This book maps out the carbon footprint of pretty much everything, from sending an email and streaming a film on Netflix to launching a space shuttle. If you don't have it already, grab a copy and familiarise yourself with the CO_2 emissions you and your business are generating.

HOW CO$_2$ EMISSIONS OR (CO2E) STACK UP

Having a one-hour Zoom call on a 13 inch MacBook Pro:	2g CO2e
Flying one person business class from Europe to Hong Kong for a meeting:	10 tonnes CO2e
Producing 600g of mens' cotton jeans:	19 kg CO2e
Flying Space X Falcon 9 to the International Space Station:	600 tonnes CO2e
Emissions from the 2019 Australian bushfires:	923 million tonnes CO2e
The annual global military carbon footprint:	3.3 billion tonnes CO2e

SOURCE: How Bad are Bananas?' Mike Berners Lee (Profile Books, 2020)

Green-proof your products

However brilliantly designed or desired your products may be, you need to look beyond these metrics and assess how ethically sound they are. Consider the following:

→ How sustainable are their component parts?

→ How ethical is the production process? Are associated workers paid a living wage?

→ What is the lifecycle of each product?

→ How can they be disposed of once they are beyond use? Can they be recycled, fully or partially?

"We are the first generation to be able to end poverty, and the last generation that can take steps to avoid the worst impacts of climate change.

Future generations will judge us harshly if we fail to uphold our moral and historical responsibilities."

Ban Ki-moon
Secretary-General, United Nations

Write an ethical manifesto

Once you understand what needs to change, you can create a public-facing manifesto. This acts as a summary of the ethical principles that drive your business, against which you can hold yourself accountable.

Make sure you include your approach to ethical decision making, environmental issues, inclusion and diversity. Map out your business principles and, if appropriate, include a five- or ten-year plan for your ethical goals, along with the improvements you will make to achieve them.

Publish your manifesto online as part of your company website and remember to review it regularly.

2. Engage your stakeholders

Having viewed your business through an ethical lens, and assembled your manifesto, you should be ready to take action. This means leading by example and empowering your stakeholders to do the same.

Your team

From everyday behaviour within the office, factory or warehouse to business travel and commuting, encourage your team to reflect on how their actions affect the environment. Ask them for their thoughts on the steps you can take, collectively and as individuals, to change things for the better.

Your shareholders

Help your shareholders understand your ethical approach, explaining why you feel it is worth any potential impact on profit. This will hopefully persuade them to become more proactive about helping to avert climate change and become more community-minded. It may even encourage them to change their own behaviour.

Supporting your community

Recent studies at Harvard and University College London have proved that people who are more connected to their community are happier, have a better sense of wellbeing, are physically healthier and live longer than people who are less well connected.

Talk to your team about the issues that are important to them. Consider allowing employees time during their office hours to champion ethical initiatives, or to work on company-funded community-based charitable projects.

If you are unsure where to start, we heartily recommend the United Nations' Global Citizen charity, which is working to address the critical issues of climate change, equality and poverty. We're so impressed by this organisation that we're donating 25% of the profits of this book to them.

3. Avoid meaningless gestures

As we noted back in 'Shifts in Thinking: 1 - Purpose', there's a noticeable rise in businesses making statements or producing results that appear to be environmentally driven. Sadly, on closer inspection, these often don't measure up.

As a BBOP, transparency should be your watchword; meaningless gestures and greenwashing have no place in a purpose-driven business.

That doesn't mean you won't face ethical challenges, but you should be open about them, and take action to address these as quickly as possible. And if you can't fix them immediately, map out a timeline by which you can – and stick to it.

Similarly, you should avoid carbon offsetting without changing environment-harming processes. As environmental consultant Adam Bastock says:

'Don't just plant trees. If you're doing tree planting just because it's cheap and easy, you're not environmentally friendly. Carbon offsetting in this way needs to be done within a context of... reductions and collaborations. Simply paying for trees and carrying on as usual is one of the worst things you can be doing.'

4. Do what you can

Today, more than 80% of the world's population live in countries that are using more resources than their ecosystems can regenerate. We are using the equivalent of 1.6 Earths to provide the resources we use and absorb our waste, which means it takes the Earth one year and eight months to regenerate what we use in a year.

As we explained in 'Shifts in Thinking: Shift 7', we firmly believe that this ecological deficit can be turned around, as long as we all play our part. When you're leading a BBOP, playing your part can have an incremental effect.

We'd suggest you take a look at The Prince's Responsible Business Network, launched over 40 years ago by the Prince of Wales, and still as relevant today. It champions *'better ways of doing business'*, backed up by a website that offers resources on everything from tackling modern-day slavery to building links with your local community.

Here are another couple of initiatives to inspire you into action:

→ **The seaweed revolution**

Seaweed, like Kelp, uses photosynthesis to turn carbon dioxide (CO_2) into seaweed biomass, a process known as carbon sequestration. Seaweed grows incredibly fast, and so can absorb CO_2 at a phenomenal rate; so supporting kelp forests would directly offset your CO_2.

Check out the Sussex Kelp Restoration Project, a pioneering marine rewilding project working to restore 200 square kilometres of lost kelp forest along the coast of Sussex.

→ **Trees and communities**

UK charity TreeSisters funds a diverse portfolio of community-led tropical reforestation projects, aiming to expand natural forest cover and avoid further deforestation. So far, it has funded the planting of over 18 million trees across 12 locations in Brazil, Borneo, Cameroon, India, Kenya, Mozambique, Madagascar, Nepal and West Papua.

By supporting local communities, improving livelihoods, protecting critically endangered species and focusing on gender parity and the participation of women, they offer a direct and measurable way to restore the web of life and mitigate climate change.

Remember what Adam Bastock said; initiatives such as these need to sit within the context of environmentally positive processes. Here are his recommendations for getting this right:

→ **Reduce.** Instead of just replacing your existing processes or products with eco-alternatives, try to reduce your total consumption overall. It is far easier to use less energy than it is to ensure that the energy is 100% renewable. Even eco-friendly products will have carbon footprints attached.

→ **Collaborate.** Most of your carbon emissions will be in your supply chain and come from other businesses you work with. So having sought to work with others who share your environmental principles, support each other to make progress.

→ **Influence.** Especially for service businesses, influence is the biggest impact they can have. Showing other businesses the benefits of being more environmentally friendly could have a much bigger impact than a reduction in your own emissions.

Above all, don't see your ethical activities as a cost; see them as an investment in future-proofing your business, your team, your community and your planet.

In short

If you're leading a BBOP, you need to be completely across the ethical impact of your business, and to consider the positive change that you can leave as your legacy.

That means exploring the effect you're currently having on the planet and the communities who live on it, and taking steps to improve it. It means getting your team and shareholders on board, and choosing to work with suppliers who share your values and can amplify your impact.

Ultimately, we hope that all businesses will put back more than they take from the planet, but don't be daunted by the size of that task. Take steps to improve every aspect of your own business and contribute to the global movement for greater good.

A note on B-Corp certification

Launched by B Lab in the early 2000s, B Corp certification helps mission-driven companies protect and improve their positive impact over time. Being certified as a B Corp tells the world that your business is meeting the highest standards of verified performance, from your supply chain and input materials to your charitable giving and employee benefits.

What does certification involve?

Certification is done mostly online, with 10% of applications selected for a more thorough review. The process includes the following:

→ A B Impact Assessment. This measures your company's social and environmental performance and uses these metrics to evaluate how your company's entire operations and business model affect your workers, community, environment, and customers.

→ A *'Declaration of Interdependence'*, committing you to using business as a force for good. Company directors must *'consider stakeholders besides shareholders in company decision-making'*. Information on *'any sensitive practices, fines, and sanctions related to the company or its partners'* must be disclosed.

→ There are also some transparency and accountability requirements, designed to guarantee that your business will have a positive impact. The certification process requires you to build your environmental and social agenda into your company's legal structure, committing you to consider stakeholder impact over the long term.

Companies must re-certify every three years.

Is it worth it?

It's only right to acknowledge that the B Corp concept isn't perfect. In particular, we believe that the company should create a directory of organisations that have lost their B Corp status. Certified businesses can choose to de-certify themselves at any time, so there should be a way of tracking whether those who have benefitted from the brand value of certification are still living up to their commitments.

We also believe that the certifying body should be completely transparent and make all the knowledge they have collected public. It's always problematic when a certifying body self-monitors its own standards; sharing this knowledge would make B Corp's certification a more reliable method for confirming that businesses are adhering to the standards they demand.

On balance, however, we strongly believe that B Corp certification is a force for good in the world. So is it something you should contemplate? That largely depends on whether you are established enough to make it viable.

For some start-ups and smaller businesses, becoming B Corp certified may just be too much to take on, and too expensive to implement on top of your day-to-day company fire-fighting. But for those of you who are more established, being aware of the core principles that B Lab champion, and starting to apply them to your business, is a positive step on the path to becoming a BBOP.

6.4 Planet: jump off points

Questions to spur you into action

→ What is the environmental impact of your business? What could you do to improve it?

→ Could you collaborate with suppliers whose ethics and production methods match your own?

→ Each time you sell a product, could you make a donation to your chosen charity?

→ What initiatives could you support in your community?

→ Could your team offer your specialist expertise to a local youth group or nature reserve?

→ How can you and your BBOP contribute to changing our ecological deficit into a surplus?

NOW RE-SCORE YOURSELF ON THE PQUALIZER

7 PLATFORMS

7.1 Platforms: From limited impact to levers of growth

Platforms are points of leverage. Be smart with technology to differentiate your business and do your heavy lifting for growth. Tech isn't the only platform out there; you can use creativity and partnerships in this way, as well as the other 6 Ps. When you do, you'll create breathing space and thinking time for the people in your organisation to focus on your purpose, and succeed at scale.

What we'll explore

1. What it looks like when you get platforms right

2. The impact of getting it wrong

Heads up: why being purposeful about platforms is important

Modern-day disruptors like Airbnb, Uber, Salesforce and Netflix often describe themselves as platforms, or platform-based businesses. That's because they've created businesses with little or no physical infrastructure, using technology (largely in the form of bespoke software) to generate huge leverage.

It's important to note that the concept of platforms as leverage generators is not limited to the world of tech. If we go back to the original, literal sense of the word, before the disruptors got their hands on it, a platform is *'a raised level surface on which people or things can stand'*. In short, something to make you bigger.

The scope of this P is far wider – and the impact far greater – than a tech solution. It is any point of leverage that you can use to scale up your BBOP. Helpfully, each of the other 6 Ps can operate as a platform in this way:

→ **Purpose**: by existing to make life better for others, you inspire people to gravitate towards you and help you succeed

→ **Positioning**: by positioning yourself clearly and differentiating yourself from others, you power up your marketing efforts and budget

→ **People**: by treating everyone who touches your business well, you create internal and external advocates, which drives more advocacy, more customers and more opportunity for all

→ **Product**: by aligning your product with your positioning, you drive confidence, strong pricing and good market fit, and encourage people to choose your product over alternatives

→ **Profit**: by ensuring you're commercially strong and confident for the future, you can invest and grow, which in turn allows you to build a Better Business On Purpose, and make decisions for the long term

→ **Planet**: by rooting your decisions in ethical and environmental principles, you contribute to the global movement for greater good and encourage others to do the same

But just like the unheard tree falling in the forest, if no one knows about the BBOP you're building, it's less likely to have a meaningful, positive impact. So once you're scoring consistently above 2 on all of the other Ps, increasing your score for platforms is essential.

To demonstrate the different ways that the concept of platforms can be applied to your business, we'll take you through a couple of examples.

1a. What it looks like when you get platforms right: Airbnb

In 2020, on Airbnb's first day of trading as a public company, its valuation surpassed the combined value of the world's three largest hotel chains: Hilton Worldwide Holdings, Marriott International, and Intercontinental Hotels Group.

How on earth did that happen? The answer is that three former roommates saw the potential for technology to solve a supply and demand problem, and changed the rules of the hotel game.

Rewind to 2008, when Brian Chesky and Joe Gebbia clocked that demand for San Francisco hotel rooms far outstripped supply when big conferences or other events were taking place – and saw it as an opportunity to use their extra space to make a bit of cash.

They tested out their theory around the time of the Industrial Design Conference, putting three air mattresses in their spare room and renting it out as a bed and breakfast. Bookings followed, Nathan Blecharczyk joined them to head up the technology side of things, and Airbnb was born.

The value of looking at a problem from a new perspective

There are so many interesting angles to this story (not least the fact that they originally included themselves as tour guides as part of the experience). But a critical point is that they re-evaluated the problem and used that to design their solution.

Chesky and Gebbia worked out that the supply and demand imbalance wasn't fundamentally about a lack of space; and that the solution wasn't to create more of it, or to charge more for it. Instead, they recognised that it was a marketplace problem, and developed a way to connect the people who had extra space with those who needed to borrow it.

It's worth noting, of course, that Airbnb couldn't have existed even 30 years ago, as the building blocks required to create a business of this kind (such as widespread, high-speed internet access, online shopping habits, and smartphone technology) weren't in place.

But it's too simple to say that Airbnb is successful because of technology. It's more that technology is an enabler that allows the company to meet a need they have identified – and has become such a key point of leverage that Airbnb is categorised as a platform-based business.

Today, Airbnb continues to leverage technology to better serve its customers. Like advanced AI that can recommend optimum pricing strategies or detect unique features of a property from photos. Or a bespoke and hugely advanced custom CRM that can recommend the best match based on things like a user's previous travel experiences or reviews.

And the sophistication of their **platforms**, and their impact across the business, is reflected in how we'd score the Airbnb PQualizer at the time of writing (see following page).

As we noted in our chapter about people, Airbnb were celebrated for their considerate, generous, and human approach to enforced redundancies in the wake of Covid-19. And as the travel market settles down, and the impact of going public becomes clearer, they are reporting record levels of profit, quarter on quarter.

Additionally, their **positioning** is so strong that it has seen them define and continue to dominate a new category in a hugely crowded and competitive space.

Airbnb 2021 PQualizer

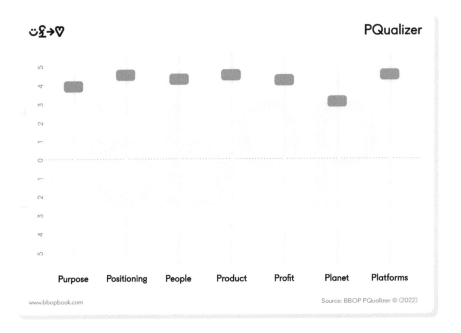

This works hand in hand with **product** innovation. Guest and host reviews are baked into the model, which helps Airbnb build an increasingly better product while deepening the trust and confidence of the user base.

Their **purpose**, *'to create a world where anyone can belong anywhere'* is clear, and continues to drive their strategy and each of the other Ps. On the surface, Airbnb's fundamental sharing economy based business model is good for the **planet**. However, more scale in the form of more stays in more Airbnbs has led to negative side effects for local communities impacting the current **planet** score.

As with all disruptive businesses, there are losers as well as winners. The impact on holiday hotspots such as Cornwall, where the long-term rental market has contracted dramatically, and tourism numbers are potentially unmanageable, has caused a great deal of soul searching. In Spain, there have been moves to tackle platform-based lettings with heavy taxes and clampdowns on unlicensed properties.

But it could be argued that this demonstrates all the more clearly how successfully Airbnb have used **platforms** to leverage their business, and deliver increasing value for new and existing customers, while also continuing to scale.

1b. What it looks like when you get platforms right: Nike

Nike have been living their call to *'Just do it'* for over 50 years. Today, the company is so established that the swoosh brand is recognised by 97% of Americans. Every man, woman and child in the US spends an average of $20 a year on the company's products.

The company's leaders have built the most valuable brand in the world, delivering consistent, profitable growth, over many years. How? By developing innovative solutions and responses across all areas of the business, which can be used to leverage success.

Like Airbnb, Nike have excelled at digital platforms, embracing technology and using it to scale their impact. The company was an early adopter of internet marketing, email management technologies, and other online communication channels which have helped to grow its reach.

But they have also embraced the concept of partnerships as a platform to leverage their impact, working with the best of the best all over the world – athletes, teams, retailers, manufacturers or supply chain providers – to serve the needs of their global customers. In 2018, Nike widened the concept of platforms even further, to dramatic effect.

When a political stance is a platform

Unlike most of their competitors, Nike don't shy away from political risk; they fully embrace it. They've shown that picking a side can turn a marketing campaign from basic awareness-building into global culture-shaping and positive change.

In 2017, NFL quarterback Colin Kaepernick began taking the knee during the national anthem, to protest about social inequality and police violence against unarmed black people. Others followed, a movement was born, and people quickly took sides, with President Trump calling for the protesting players to be fired.

When Kaepernick's contract ended, and he remained unsigned, it was widely attributed to the political stance he had taken. And while many organisations steered clear, Nike did the opposite. In 2018, they put Kaepernick at the heart of their 13th *'Just do it'* campaign.

This wasn't just a campaign. It was a bold, authentic and powerful effort to change the way minority groups are treated. It was a great example of the way Nike uses different platforms – in this case, a political one – to increase their impact.

By aligning with Kaepernick and the army of supporters and followers that he'd amassed, Nike became part of a political movement, elevating the conversation and debate. They united their platform with Kaepernick's and raised global awareness of social inequality.

Critically, this wasn't about selling shoes; it was a perfectly positioned manifestation of their purpose; to *'move the world forward through the power of sport – breaking barriers and building community to change the game for all.'*

Colin Kaepernick
@Kaepernick7

Follow

Believe in something, even if it means
sacrificing everything. #JustDolt

Believe in something. Even if it
means sacrificing everything.

8:20 PM - 3 Sep 2018

214,047 Retweet **509,003** Likes

20K   214K   509K

SOURCE: Twitter

Unsurprisingly, then, we would score Nike at the top of the scale
for **platforms**, **purpose** and **positioning** in 2019; and they show up well
across most of the other Ps too.

They are known for delivering cutting-edge **products** – their Nike Air
range, for example, was inspired by an aerospace engineer and was the first
trainer to have an air cushion in its sole.

They also treat sport itself as a product of sorts, seeing it as a universal language, which transcends cultures, borders and barriers, and changes lives.

This attitude is also visible in the way they invest **profits** into grassroots and global initiatives, supporting **people** of all ages, as well as the communities they live in.

The only one we've scored them down on is **planet**. Because while it's true that they have made commitments to sustainability, zero carbon and zero waste, no global high-street fashion brand can realistically score more than 1 due to the sheer volume of stuff they produce.

Nike 2019 PQualizer

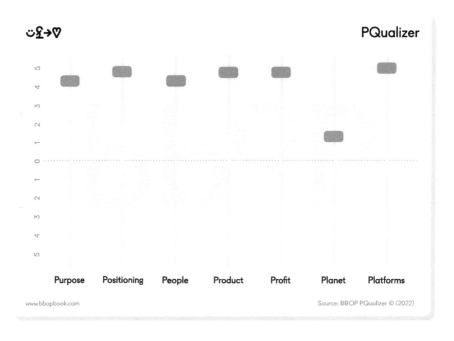

2. The impact of getting it wrong

Unfortunately, BBOP founders often get stuck when it comes to platforms. Why? Because building them tends to involve up-front investment, as well as a healthy dose of risk-taking and long-term thinking. When you're building your business, it can be hard to get off the treadmill and focus on how to work **on** it, rather than **in** it.

There's also a clear tension between making a difference at a relatively small, localised level versus dialling up platforms to scale the business. Not every founder wants to scale, and that's OK. But when you're building a BBOP, everyone benefits when you grow; scaling something good can make it truly great.

In Brighton, where we all live, there are some brilliant organisations that haven't ratcheted up platforms to a point where they're known more widely. That's a shame, because they're doing great things.

Take HISBE, which stands for *'How It Should Be'*. It's a community interest company (CIC) that is setting out to *'transform the food industry by challenging the way big supermarkets do business',* offering a range of everyday groceries thoughtfully sourced from small, local producers and brands that trade responsibly, fairly and sustainably. As they explain:

'For you, this means healthier and more ethical options. Our suppliers get a fair price for quality products. And we can show the big supermarkets How It Should Be.'

Currently, HISBE have two rebel supermarkets. People love them, and they've proven the business model; they've developed a Bootcamp strategy, where they work with and train other rebel shops and food brands to follow in their footsteps. But just imagine what they could achieve if they leveraged a range of platforms to scale up further.

In short

BBOPs set out to make the world better. But without scaling up, they won't be able to have the same impact. That's where platforms come in.

Platforms are essentially anything that can give you an edge; so invest in them early, and often. You don't have to do it alone; you could consider franchise models, partnerships with larger and value-aligned companies or sharing your blueprint with others in territories or markets that you're not able to reach.

Keep an open mind about what makes a point of leverage; remember, creativity, technology, partnerships and all of the other Ps can act as platforms for your business. It's this mix of multiple points of leverage that creates both scalability and longevity.

7.2 Score your Platforms

SCORE YOUR ORGANISATION FOR
POSITIONING USING THE BBOP PQUALIZER

Are you using multiple points of leverage to scale your positive impact and generate sustainable growth?

5	Your platforms are helping your business scale and thrive at pace.
3	You have platforms in place, but there is still work to be done to optimise their impact.
1	Your thinking on platforms is underway.
0	Your platforms are not established.
-1	Your operating processes are manual rather than automated in most instances, causing inefficiency and ineffectiveness.
-3	A lack of platforms is holding you back, making it hard to create meaningful impact.
-5	Your organisation is at risk due to a lack of platforms, and no scalable business model.

7.3 Platforms in Action

Having explored the different platforms that leverage growth, from technology and partnerships to the other 6 Ps, we will now show you how to put these platforms to work, so you can scale up your BBOP and maximise the positive impact you can make in the world.

Five steps to shift your approach to platforms

1. Make sure your Ps are balanced
2. Invest in design and communications
3. Embrace technology – but not at the expense of people
4. Get comfortable with AI
5. Build a set of core tech tools

1. Make sure your Ps are balanced

Before you start trying to scale your products or services, you need to make sure they're worth the effort; there's little point in trying to share something inferior with the world. That, as you have hopefully grasped by this point in the book, means making sure the other 6 Ps are in line.

If you haven't already done so, go back and score your company on the PQualizer, and use the previous chapters to help you bring everything to line. Then you're ready to start using the other platforms to leverage your business.

2. Invest in design and communications

Your impact will be all the greater if you're communicating what you want to say clearly, purposefully and enticingly. It's not just what you say that counts, it's how you say it; and that's as true for internal comms as it is for outward-facing campaigns.

Take care with your communications; make them enjoyable to read, easy to understand, and straightforward to respond to. Similarly, make sure you understand and value the role of design as a way to showcase your product or service, and show what you stand for. That includes behavioural and user experience design, as well as the purely visual sense.

This isn't just relevant to big-ticket campaigns; every point of contact with a customer or colleague is an opportunity to illustrate your purpose. Our favourite example of this is CD Baby, a company founded by Derek Sivers back in 1998 to help musicians to make and distribute their CDs to their fans. Search *private CD baby jet* to see how Sivers delighted his audience – and the impact this had.

As Sivers' example shows, being creative with your design and communications, whilst making sure that they align with your brand and your purpose, will make what you're trying to say all the more powerful. If you don't have the skills in-house, bring them in, or find a partner or supplier who does.

3. Embrace technology – but not at the expense of people

As we've noted, technology isn't the only platform a business has at its disposal; but there's no arguing that both hardware and software can be massive points of leverage.

A good way to look at it is that technology acts as a multiplier of your abilities. To give a practical example, if you're looking to scale your business, you're likely to be operating in multiple locations, with different time zones, languages and currencies. Achieving this without technology is pretty much impossible.

Similarly, technology that's been designed and embedded well within your BBOP drives efficiency, process and structure, leading to a better and more consistent quality of service.

However, as a BBOP, you do need to make sure that embracing the upsides of technology doesn't mean you ignore the downsides – specifically, that your people don't pay the price.

Striking a balance between humans and robots

There's no question that a growing number of jobs are being automated, and that this is frightening for those who are deemed replaceable. For a BBOP, with a responsibility to do the right thing by all stakeholders (including employees, partners and suppliers) this is a difficult one to balance.

But simply pretending this isn't happening, King Canute style, is no better than letting it happen unchecked. Instead, you should embrace the change, and take an active decision to fit the solution to the situation, using technology where that's the right thing to do, and people when they're the best fit.

Technology is great for predictable and monotonous rule-based tasks, but awful at storytelling, imagination and vision, critical thinking, creative problem solving, dealing with nuance, empathy and communication or uncertainty... all areas where people excel. Technology also can't compete physically with humans, particularly for tasks requiring high degrees of dexterity in a foreign environment.

This is all very well in principle, of course, but what happens when a particular technology reaches a tipping point making jobs or relationships redundant? The answer is to tackle it head-on, in a way that has your people's interests at heart.

To use a real-life example, let's take DHL, whose drivers are 25% more effective than their competitors, thanks to the sophisticated route planning they use. At this point, technology is helping leverage success. But in the next three years, developments in autonomous driving technology are likely to fundamentally disrupt the sector, with people not needed at the wheel for much of the driving.

A BBOP response to this would be to look for opportunities within the company that drivers could start re-skilling towards. Or to lobby and work with local government to initiate and support any re-skilling that might need to happen beyond the company. These questions would help with this process:

→ What other roles in your organisation might be suitable for drivers, with some additional training?

→ What other organisations might be a good match for their skills or experience, with some additional training?

→ What else could drivers be doing while sitting in a vehicle but not driving?

→ Does this change mean that a single driver could reasonably 'drive' for longer periods?

→ What modifications could you make to your vehicles to make this change more pleasant and effective for our drivers?

→ How will this change play out in the medium to long term?

It's a question of balance; instead of prioritising technology at the expense of all else, a BBOP should be seeking to balance it with people's needs. To apply the DHL principles more generally, that means:

→ Dedicating time to focus on potential innovation within your market and its potential impact on your people, looking three years ahead.

→ Exploring the new technology to understand its capabilities and shortcomings.

→ Taking responsibility for mitigating the impact on your people, and working with others to initiate and support alternative solutions.

The one exception to embracing technology

There is one kind of business that doesn't need to take the same approach to technology. In a world of mass production, many customers crave something more unique, imperfect even; and artisan businesses fulfil this need, producing limited quantities, often using traditional methods.

If this is your market, embrace it, and celebrate your point of difference. That doesn't mean rejecting technology altogether – you should still invest in excellent, scalable e-commerce solutions, CRM systems and outbound sales channels, for example. But the production side of things can retain a more crafting-based focus.

Hiut Denim Company are a brilliant example of how to do this well; you can read more about them in 'Shifts in Thinking: Shift 2'.

4. Get comfortable with AI

AI, or Artificial Intelligence, is a new technology with a scary reputation, largely as a result of the media spin and hype around it. Like other new advances in tech, it is set to disrupt business as usual; in fact, it's already started. Just as it's now hard to imagine any business operating without the internet, the same will increasingly become the case with AI.

BBOPs need to get to grips with AI, and use it purposefully. So what exactly is it, and how can it help your business?

A good way to think of AI in its current form is as an *'idiot savant'*; that is, an entity that is highly knowledgeable about one subject but knows little about anything else, and has no common sense.

The AI process involves feeding huge amounts of data into an algorithm, which 'learns' by looking for patterns in the data, in the same way that the human brain learns. But while these algorithms are incredibly effective in isolation, they can't identify nuance, and can't collaborate.

For example, let's imagine that you feed an AI lots of pictures of tigers, and tell the algorithm that these images represent tigers. With enough pictures and accurate classification, you'll have a very fast and very accurate method of tiger identification.

You might then assume that if you then feed it lots of pictures of cats, along with supporting data that these images are not tigers, the AI would be able to correctly identify cats; but that's not how it works. To achieve that, you'd need to go through the same process of specifically telling the AI that these pictures represent cats; it can't make that link itself.

Essentially, then, AI is most useful as a way to carry out complex but non-nuanced tasks that don't require any common sense; tasks that are slow and expensive to complete. The good news is, you won't need a PhD in AI to capitalise on it, as it's now easily accessible through many cloud-based services.

For example, Amazon's AWS AI services include capabilities such as demand forecasting, real-time translation and image and video analysis. IBM Watson, Google Cloud and Microsoft Azure AI provide similar services. More and more cloud-based tech providers are building in AI capability; Salesforce's new *Einstein* feature can accurately predict things like sales churn and future lifetime value.

5. Build a set of core tech tools

Whilst you'll need to match your tech to your business's specific needs, sector and scale, there are a number of core software products that every BBOP should invest in. Ideally, they should be mobile-enabled, to give you maximum flexibility.

To help you get started, we've put together an illustrative list, including some well-known and widely adopted products. They are all cloud-based, SaaS products, which means:

→ They don't require any physical infrastructure

→ They will be straightforward to roll out

→ They can operate on a global level

→ They can be swapped out for an alternative if your needs change

→ They have high levels of redundancy and availability baked in, making your systems and data reliable and easy to access.

A business command centre

Businesses are like complex machines which makes consistency difficult, especially at scale. But customers want predictable and consistent products or services. Just as a train needs rails to keep it on track, so does your business.

There's a reason why hospitals have protocols for everything; they enable multiple staff to give consistent care to a single patient, minimising human error. In a hospital setting, not following the protocol can be a matter of life and death. In a business setting, it can be similarly dangerous for stability.

In the earlier stages of business growth, you can define key processes, then create 'playbooks' which explain them simply enough for someone with the right skills to follow. But as your business scales, these playbooks will become increasingly complex and varied, often requiring collaboration and cross-department communication.

This is the point where you need to invest in software that will enable you to put your business processes on rails, by allowing you to design new business processes and alter existing ones. It should also offer management information that enables leaders to proactively resolve any bottlenecks early, and give real-time insight into your business's performance.

Try to use the same product across different departments and business units. Good examples are Trello, Jobber, Basecamp, JIRA, Salesforce, WorkFlowMax and Asana.

Communication software

Every business needs effective channels for both internal and external communications. For BBOPs, who value and invest in relationships with their stakeholders, they're all the more important.

Even in this era of voice notes and instant messaging, nothing beats the simplicity of a voice call, so make sure you have decent phone systems in place. Cloud-based, virtual systems such as Ring Central are now highly sophisticated, offering much more than traditional phone systems at a much lower cost. Or it may be simpler, and more effective, for your team, to use their mobile phones.

Other key communication platforms include:

→ **Email systems** that work everywhere, don't limit attachments and have plenty of capacity. Gmail or Office365 are good examples.

→ **Messaging solutions** such as Slack, that allow short-form communication and sharing of files and information. You'll need to be clear with your people about when and how to use this rather than email and other channels.

→ You may also want something similar, enabled on your website, for use with your customers and partners. Intercom is currently the gold standard, but there are plenty of others including Crisp, an independent alternative.

→ **Video-based communications and collaboration solutions,** which came into their own during the pandemic, and are still very much in use in the hybrid working world. Choose one that's easy for anyone in the business to use anywhere; good examples are Zoom, Google Meet and Whereby.

→ NoHQ's website has guides to the tools and tactics used by the most effective remote working companies, which are helpful reading for any BBOP looking to build better remote working teams.

Finance software

Every business needs software that provides reliable, real-time financial data, and makes it easy for customers to pay you, and for other businesses to do business with you. You should also make sure your finance software can:

→ **Automate chasing of debtors** – but make sure you incorporate humility and personality. Even chasing a late payer is an opportunity to make a meaningful connection.

→ **Pay everyone on time** – obvious, perhaps, but mission-critical for a company that cares about its people.

→ **Give early warning indicators** for situations requiring action. For example, cash falling below a given threshold; currency fluctuations above or below given thresholds; late payers beyond a given period; over-dependence on one or more customers.

➜ **Deliver automated reports** that give you a snapshot of how finance relates to your current business KPIs. For example, if you've just opened up a new sales territory, you might want weekly reports showing its total revenue, number of customers, lifetime value and churn.

Good examples include Xero and Salesforce.

Legal software

Many people find legal documents intimidating, so it's important to make them as easy to access and understand as possible.

Online tools like Docusign can help simplify contract signing and approval processes, and make paper copies unnecessary. Don't be afraid of introducing warmth and personality into any emails or other text that support your legal documents; it demystifies the process and makes it feel more personal.

Documents

Limiting your use of paper is good for the planet, and online documentation platforms have a lot to offer. So save paper for getting thoughts out of your head, and for doodling and sketching, and use digital tools for everything else.

This entire book was written in Notion, which made discussion, collaboration and approval incredibly easy. Other popular examples are Gsuite and Office365.

People

The more you scale, the more people you'll employ, and the harder it will be to look after them all properly. The right software can help you do it well.

There are tools available to manage and track every part of the HR process, from job ads, hiring and onboarding to developing and supporting people's careers. And the remuneration side of things can be taken care of with simple, but sophisticated, payroll and benefits software.

Good examples are Gusto, CharlieHR and BreatheHR.

The small stuff

Look for opportunities to automate repetitive and time-wasting processes and encourage your team to use them. This will remove mundane jobs from their workload, freeing them up for more interesting and impactful activities.

Two good examples of this are scheduling and security. Products like Calendly can remove a lot of the toing and froing involved in finding convenient times. Tools such as 1Password can eliminate both the timewasting and security risk caused by lost and forgotten logins.

Just imagine what your people could achieve in the time this kind of automation gave them back.

In short

Invest time, money and thought into building platforms that will streamline your processes and multiply your abilities. These include well-crafted design, creativity and communication, innovative technology, and the other 6 Ps.

Look ahead to see where the technology that's relevant to your market is headed, and take action to prepare for and implement it. Understand the impact this might have on your people, and take steps to help them develop alternative futures.

Ultimately, platforms enable you to scale the positive impact that your BBOP is making, in the most efficient, effective and purposeful way. Use them well.

7.4 Platforms: jump off points

Questions to spur you into action

→ Are your Ps in balance?

→ What other points of leverage could help you scale your business?

→ What are the likely technological developments that will affect your business in the next three years? What will the impact be on your people?

→ What impact will advances in AI have on your business in the short, medium and long term?

→ What technology could you use to streamline different parts of your business, and look after and develop your people?

**NOW RE-SCORE YOURSELF
ON THE PQUALIZER**

"Evil doesn't have to be an overt act; it can be merely the absence of good. If you have the ability, the resources, and the opportunity to do good and you do nothing, that can be evil."

Yvon Chouinard

SECTION 3

CONCLUSION

We wrote this book because we want to change the world.

You've just read it, which means, like us, you also want to change the world.

Firstly, thank you for investing your time in exploring our ideas. Secondly, ideas are just that. Without action they remain as just ideas.

That's not the point of this book.

Now is your time.

It's been great to share our thinking with you. As we shared at the start – people created business, not the other way around – we don't need to become slaves to the balance sheet. Therein lies the rub, it's all about balance. There are many points of inspiration to achieve it – taking a leaf from some of the case studies we've shared, including:

- Buurtzorg, who revolutionised a national health system, resulting in better patient outcomes.

- Patagonia and Lego, who are driving the green agenda in a way that brings people with them.

- Dogma by Pedigree, who turned their business around by thinking creatively about their customers.

- Apple, whose commitment to product innovation has changed the way people interact with the world and each other – more than once.

Take on board the shifts in thinking and doing to help you create more balance. You'll be able to run your business without it running you, while making profit with pride to fuel your purpose.

Just as Nile Rodgers at the Amsterdam Dance Event once said, 'Music without soul is just noise'.

As we said earlier in this book: business without purpose is just admin – and life, quite frankly, is far too short for that.

It's hard to challenge norms. But if you've got this far then we believe in your ability to take action. You know there's not a choice. You know you've only got so much time to make a difference. You know that that difference is baked into your DNA.

So own it.

One last thing.

Remember: you're not on your own.

There are thousands of other BBOP leaders helping to create the positive change and impact that we're all looking for. Let's help each other as much as possible.

Sometimes changing to becoming a fully-fledged BBOP requires external impetus. And it goes without saying that if you'd benefit from that in your journey towards becoming a BBOP, please do get in touch.

Nikki   *Tim.*

Neil

Connect with the authors:

Neil Witten

Pigs In Flight Ltd

🌐 www.neil.land

in www.linkedin.com/in/neilwitten

🐦 @nwitten

Nikki Gatenby

Gatenbys Consulting Ltd

🌐 www.superengaged.co.uk

in www.linkedin.com/in/nikkigatenby

🐦 @NikkiGatenby

Tim Healey

Shoot 4 The Moon Ltd

🌐 www.shoot4themoon.co.uk

in www.linkedin.com/in/timhealey

🐦 @timhealey

THANKS

The authors would like to thank:

Editor Cathy Halstead, without whose patience, good-humoured kicks and dedication to our work none of this would be possible.

Creative Director Wayne Fick, whose keen visual-eye shaped our book cover, layout and website.

Jo Humphreys and Shan Healey who painstakingly applied razor-sharp focus to our proofreading

Ali Dewji for stellar advice on and around the completion of our book and bringing it to life.

Danish creative agency Worth Your While, who delivered our BBOP logo and cypher.

All of our supporters whose enthusiasm for our book helped bring it to life.

Tim Healey would like to thank:

Fiona Cullen, for the faith you have had in me to see this project through.

Rob Day, for guidance, reference and input.

My daughters, Suki and Coco, who are my inspiration.

Nikki Gatenby would like to thank:

Justine Katherine, for encouragement, support and the occasional good-humoured reminder that it was all going to be worth the hours of thinking, writing and editing – particularly when I said I'd never write another book!

Ian Harris, Carla Heath, Simon Collard, Sally-Anne Airey and Daniel de la Cruz, for their brutal honesty on our few first thoughts, including the title when we couldn't see the wood for the trees. Invaluable.

My husband, Neale, for making me laugh, no matter what is going on. And mum and dad, my eternal rocks. You rock.

Neil Witten would like to thank:

Tim and Nikki! Thanks for bearing with me and encouraging me to stay the course with this. Ray Richards, co-host of <u>Life Done Differently</u> and founder of Do Something Different. Because you just 'get it'.

Stuart Scott and Alex Vaidya, co-founders of my previous two companies. You made space for me to learn and to experiment in business which helped immensely to catalyse this book.

All of the conscious businesspeople (you know who you are). Your influence on the world and attitude towards business has always shaped my thinking. My forum group (again, you know who you are). You've always been there for me and helped me see what's staring me in the face, focus on what matters and hold me to account. Eddie and Dan for helping me move, and adapt. Adrian, John, Mike and all of the other early Dataline Software folks. The OGs of BBOP.

My beautiful, caring, thoughtful wife Emma, and my crazies, Ben and Sam. I'm so lucky to be able to call you my family. Russell, Mark and co (you know who you are). I love going through life with you all.

And finally, my parents. Mum, two famous quotes come to mind: 'there's no such word as can't' and 'it's not what you say, but the way you say it'. I think I finally get it. Dad, I miss you. You always saw my energy and encouraged me towards it. That's been a huge gift. Thank you. Legends. All of you.

FEEDBACK

We'd love to hear about your journey towards becoming a BBOP. What in our book has worked, and what hasn't? Which case-studies resonated, and which of our suggested initiatives yielded the best results? Please email us with your news, or indeed any questions that our book has raised for you and your business. thebook@bbop.global

Endnotes

1   https://www.patagonia.com/core-values/

2   *Let My People Go Surfing*, Yvon Chouinard, Penguin, (2016)

3   https://en.wikipedia.org/wiki/WeWork

4   https://www.responsible-investor.com/articles/deliveroo-the-worst-ipo-in-history-with-a-side-order-of-esg-investor-boycott

5   https://techcrunch.com/2020/12/21/silicon-valley-should-reward-zebras-not-unicorns/amp/?guccounter=1

6   https://www.entrepreneur.com/amphtml/322407

7   Forbes magazine on Tony's Chocolonely: https://www.forbes.com/sites/afdhelaziz/2020/10/30/how-the-netherlands-no-1-chocolate-brand-tonys-chocolonely-is-winning-fans-in-the-usand-helping-people-vote/?sh=ca9fee437b92

8   Dr Kati Kariko's story: https://www.nytimes.com/2021/04/08/health/coronavirus-mrna-kariko.html

9   https://www.pwc.co.uk/press-room/press-releases/AI-will-create-as-many-jobs-as-it-displaces-by-boosting-economic-growth.html

10 https://www.forbes.com/sites/danielshapiro1/2019/10/23/can-artificial-intelligence-think/?sh=71d38b632d7c

11 The Future Starts Here: An Optimistic Guide To What Comes Next, John Higgs, Weidenfeld & Nicolson (2019)

12   https://www.today.com/tmrw/greta-thunberg-testifies-congress-earth-day-t216009

13   Baroness Minouche Shafik's call for change: https://www.lse.ac.uk/Events/LSE-Festival/Post-Covid-World/Events/20210301/contract

14   Value(s): Building a Better World for All, Mark Carney, McClelland & Stewart, (2021)

15   Ingka Group's climate commitments: https://www.ikea.com/us/en/this-is-ikea/newsroom/ingka-group-accelerates-investment-in-transition-to-renewable-energy-with-additional-4-billion-euro-pubdcd2cdb0

16   The benefits of dog ownership: https://greatergood.berkeley.edu/article/item/the_science_backed_benefits_of_being_a_dog_owner

www.get-known.co.uk

BV - #0030 - 191222 - C0 - 229/152/17 - PB - 9781913717964 - Matt Lamination